Internet Information Services Administration

Other Books by New Riders Publishing

Planning for Windows 2000
Eric Cone, Jon Boggs, & Sergio Perez
ISBN: 0-7357-0048-6

Windows NT DNS
Michael Masterson, Herman Knief,
Scott Vinick, & Eric Roul
ISBN: 1-56205-943-2

Windows NT Network Management:
Reducing Total Cost of Ownership
Anil Desai
ISBN: 1-56205-946-7

Windows NT Performance
Monitoring, Benchmarking, & Tuning
Mark Edmead & Paul Hinsburg
ISBN: 1-56205-942-4

Windows NT Registry
Sandra Osborne
ISBN: 1-56205-941-6

Windows NT TCP/IP
Karanjit Siyan
ISBN 1-56205-887-8

Windows NT Terminal
Server & Citrix MetaFrame
Ted Harwood
ISBN: 1-56205-944-0

Cisco Router Configuration &
Troubleshooting
Mark Tripod
ISBN: 1-56205-944-0

Exchange System Administration
Janice Rice Howd
ISBN: 0-7357-0081-8

Implementing Exchange Server
Doug Hauger, Marywynne Leon,
& William C. Wade III
ISBN: 1-56205-931-9

Network Intrusion Detection:
An Analyst's Handbook
Stephen Northcutt
ISBN: 0-7357-0868-1

Understanding Data Communications,
Sixth Edition
Gilbert Held
ISBN: 0-7357-0036-2

Internet Information Services Administration

New Riders

201 West 103rd Street,
Indianapolis, Indiana 46290

Kelli Adam
with Lisa Stanley

Internet Information Services Administration

Copyright © 2000 by New Riders Publishing

International Standard Book Number: 0-7357-0022-2

Library of Congress Catalog Card Number: 99-067435

Printed in the United States of America

First Printing: *January, 2000*

04   03   02   01   00   7   6   5   4   3   2   1

Interpretation of the printing code: The rightmost double-digit number is the year of the book's printing; the rightmost single-digit number is the number of the book's printing. For example, the printing code 00-1 shows that the first printing of the book occurred in 2000.

Trademarks

Warning and Disclaimer

Publisher
David Dwyer

Executive Editor
Al Valvano

Acquisitions Editor
Amy Michaels

Product Marketing Manager
Stephanie Layton

Development Editor
Leah Williams

Managing Editor
Gina Brown

Project Editor
Elise Walter

Book Designer
Louisa Klucznik

Cover Designer
Aren Howell

Team Coordinator
Ann Quinn

Copy Editor
Krista Hansing

Indexer
Christine Karpeles

Technical Reviewers
Daniel Adam
Dan Bubb
Jon Boggs
Stephen Crandall
Mark Fitzpatrick
Jim Morey
John Thomas

Proofreader
SCAN Communications Group, Inc.

Production
SCAN Communications Group, Inc.

About the Author

Kelli Adam is currently the president and principal consultant of ConnectOS Corporation, the network consulting and Internet services firm she founded in 1995 near Redmond, Washington. She became a Microsoft Certified Professional in 1991 and went on to attain status as a Microsoft Certified Trainer and Microsoft Certified Systems Engineer Plus Internet. Kelli participated in writing Microsoft certification exams on Internet Information Server, Networking Essentials, Internet Explorer Administration Kit, Proxy Server, and SNA Server. She also coauthored *MCSE Training Guide: TCP/IP, Second Edition*, by New Riders Publishing (1-56205-920-3). Kelli taught the Microsoft train-the-trainer course on Internet Information Server in both the United States and Japan, and Proxy Server in Japan.

Most recently, Kelli was honored as one of the Top 40 executives under the age of 40 in her area. Still, she finds time to spend with her two house bunnies; her husband, Daniel; and her 1-year-old son, Nicolas. But, lately she has not found as much time to enjoy SCUBA diving, wine collecting, boating or private pilot lessons. Kelli can be reached at `KelliA@ConnectOS.com`.

About the Contributor

Lisa Stanley, MCP, is a technical engineer at ConnectOS Corporation who is responsible for technical administration of Web, SQL, and Windows Media Technology servers. Lisa's background and experience has evolved from being an intern with an associate's degree in information technology into playing an integral role in the technical success of ConnectOS. She enjoys science fiction books and movies, as well as various arts and crafts.

About the Technical Reviewers

Daniel Adam is the lead program manager for Microsoft's Windows Media Solutions & Applications Group as part of the streaming media division. In his nine years at Microsoft, Daniel spent three years as a senior consultant in the consulting services division. After that, he joined the consumer systems division working on media products, such as Interactive TV and NetShow, now known as Windows Media Technology. Daniel is currently working on Microsoft's new online pay-per-view technology. In his limited spare time, Daniel enjoys boating and is married to Kelli Adam.

Jon Boggs, MCSE, CNE, is a Senior Consultant for the eBusiness Networks practice of Xpedior in Chicago. He has provided consulting services to a number of nationally known corporations. He is an expert at automating administrative tasks and system deployments, typically employing a mix of Windows NT/2000, SMS, and Visual Basic. Jon has previously coauthored *Planning for Windows 2000*, and has served as a technical reviewer on several BackOffice-related books. He enjoys reading and biking in his spare time.

Dan Bubb owns Gorge Networks, Inc., an ISP in northern Oregon, where the bulk of his time is spent maintaining the company's network infrastructure and 300-plus Web sites. Gorge Networks is an NT-based Web hosting facility where e-commerce, fault tolerance/recovery, and scaling and capacity planning are part of every day. Dan has developed training and education material for many MS Internet applications, such as IIS, Proxy, Site Server, and Commerce Server. Dan received a liberal arts degree from the College of Idaho in 1983, and a masters of science degree in mathematics in 1987 from Oregon State University.

Steve Crandall is a technology consultant in Cleveland, Ohio, and a graduate student in the History of Science and Technology program at Case Western Reserve University. He is a columnist for *Microsoft Certified Professional Magazine*, and has contributed to books and seminars on technology topics.

Jim Crawford is a Seattle-based Web developer whose work emphasizes streaming media, distance learning, and database implementation.

Mark Fitzpatrick (markfitz@fitzme.com) is a Microsoft Most Valuable Professional (MVP) who specializes in Microsoft Internet technologies and products, such as FrontPage, Visual Interdev, and Internet Information Server. He has five years of experience designing commercial Web sites. When he isn't writing, Mark can be found in the role of Director of Technology for the Inner Reach Corporation (http://www.innerreach.com). He also runs his own Web design firm, Fitzme, Inc. (http://www.fitzme.com).

Jim Morey's interest in computers goes back to 1980, having owned a Commodore 64, Mac LC3, and several PCs. He joined the IIS team around Beta 3, and has been there through the RTM of Windows 2000, writing the security documentation for IIS 5.0 along with several Web articles on security.

John P. Thomas is the managing partner of Thomas Consulting, LLC, an Internet consulting and Web development firm established in 1994. Thomas Consulting specializes in helping organizations determine the most effective ways to incorporate Internet technologies into their operations. Thomas is the instructor for Bellevue Community College Continuing Education advanced HTML and database integration classes. In addition to being a Microsoft Certified Professional, he was the lead writer for two MCP exams: Internet Explorer 4.0 Administration Kit and FrontPage 98. Additional information is available at http://www.jthomas.com.

This book is dedicated to the two most prevalent people in my life, both now and during its writing—my son, Nicolas, and my sister, Nicole.

Acknowledgments

I've learned recently that it takes a lot of time and dedication to write a book, but it also takes a lot of support. I need to thank my technical reviewers, contributors, editors, and several friends at Microsoft for answering those annoying little questions that only someone at Microsoft could answer.

I also want to thank my family, Daniel and Nicolas, for allowing me to spend late evenings at a computer instead of with them—and, of course, my Mom and Dad, who gave me the foundation that would some day allow me to fulfill my dream of getting my name on the cover of a book. I also thank everyone at my office who understood why my door was closed more often than usual, especially Michelle for helping with some little marketing efforts that I always needed help with.

Finally, I want to thank Al and Amy for first recognizing my potential to write an insightful book on Internet Information Services, and Leah for guiding me through it.

Your Feedback Is Valuable

As the reader of this book, *you* are our most important critic and commentator. We value your opinion and want to know what we're doing right, what we could do better, what areas you'd like to see us publish in, and any other words of wisdom you're willing to pass our way.

As the Executive Editor for the Networking team at New Riders Publishing, I welcome your comments. You can fax, email, or write me directly to let me know what you did or didn't like about this book—as well as what we can do to make our books stronger.

Please note that I cannot help you with technical problems related to the topic of this book, and that due to the high volume of mail I receive, I might not be able to reply to every message.

When you write, please be sure to include this book's title and author, as well as your name and phone or fax number. I will carefully review your comments and share them with the author and editors who worked on the book.

Fax:	317-581-4663
Email:	editors@newriders.com
Mail:	Al Valvano
	Executive Editor
	New Riders Publishing
	201 West 103rd Street
	Indianapolis, IN 46290 USA

Contents

1 Installing and Managing IIS   1
Before Installation   2
System Requirements   2
Security Preview   5
Organizing Content   6
Installation   7
Managing Internet Information Services   8
Backups   10

2 Internetworking Considerations   11
Hosting Options   12
DNS Configuration   14
Handling Capacity Requirements   18

3 Integrating IIS with Windows 2000 Security   25
Windows 2000 Security Recommendations   27
User and Group Accounts   27
NTFS   30
Auditing and Logging   32
Security Planning   34

4 IIS Security   35
Internet Information Services Security with Windows 2000   35
IP Address and Domain Name Restrictions   37
Access Permissions   39
Authentication   41
Impersonation   47

5 Customizing WWW Sites   51
Under the Hood of HTTP   52
Organization of Sites   53
Operators   58
Home Directory   59
Host Headers   62
Server Extensions   66

6 **Customizing the FTP Service   69**
FTP Architecture   **70**
FTP Site Properties   **71**
Security Accounts   **73**
Home Directory   **76**
FTP Virtual Directories   **79**
Step-by-Step Setup   **80**

7 **Running Web Applications   81**
Applications and Internet Information Services   **82**
Configuring MIME Types   **84**
ISAPI Applications   **84**
ASP Applications   **85**
Creating a Web Application   **87**

8 **Microsoft FrontPage Server Extensions   93**
Installing FrontPage 2000 Server Extensions   **94**
Configuring FrontPage 2000 Extensions   **97**
Administering FrontPage 2000 Server Extensions   **98**
Security Issues with FrontPage   **99**
Connecting to a FrontPage Web   **100**
Integration with Other Services   **101**

9 **SSL and Certificate Services   103**
An Overview of the Secure Sockets Layer (SSL)   **103**
Encrypting Communication   **104**
Client Certificate Mapping   **105**
Server Certificates and Certificate Authorities   **108**
Installing and Configuring Certificate Services   **110**

10 **IIS SMTP Service and NNTP Service   113**
How SMTP Works   **114**
SendMail Components   **115**
Other Mail Solutions   **117**
SMTP Site Properties   **117**
NNTP Service   **119**

11   Connecting to Databases   123

   Microsoft Data Access Components   **124**

   How to Make the Connection   **126**

   Microsoft SQL Server versus Access   **131**

   Version Checking   **131**

   Security Issues   **132**

12   Managing Log Files   133

   Understanding Log File Formats   **133**

   Generating Reports from Log Files   **137**

   Managing Log Files   **141**

13   Performance Tuning and Reliability   143

   Optimizing Web Site Performance   **144**

   Running Applications   **146**

   Using Performance Monitor   **148**

   Editing the Registry to Improve Performance   **151**

   Improving ASP Functionality   **151**

   Load Testing   **151**

   Index   **155**

Introduction

Over the last few years, I've found an abundance of books that answer the question, "What *can* I do when administering Internet Information Server?" But I have yet to find a book that answers the more pertinent question: "What *should* I do when administering Internet Information Services?" This is the question I attempt to answer in this book.

During the course of this book, I highlight the pros and cons of many of the options available in Internet Information Services, while not actually covering the details of some of these options. These details are covered in other books and, of course, in the product documentation. I try to explain which options make sense in which situations, and why. This book also provides many recommendations based on my experience with the current version of Internet Information Services, as well as my past experience with each previous version. Most of these recommendations are also targeted at small Internet service providers (ISPs), because this is the environment in which I work. Still, the majority of the information in this book applies to all environments in which Internet Information Services could be installed, whether by a small ISP, a large ISP, or a corporate intranet.

Who Should Read This Book?

This book is written for experienced Web server administrators who intend to either upgrade to or migrate to Internet Information Services 5. It is also an excellent reference for the first-time Internet Information Services administrator, although it is not intended to be an exhaustive reference on the product. It also can be an invaluable tool for anyone planning to start a Web hosting company.

What Is Covered in This Book?

The following is a brief overview of the chapters in this book:

- **Chapter 1: "Installing and Managing IIS."** Chapter 1 starts by providing a list of questions to consider before installing Internet Information Services. The majority of the chapter focuses on making recommendations for installing Internet Information Services, including hardware and software needed, security planning, and organizing content. This chapter also includes a survey of management options and a discussion of backup options.

- **Chapter 2: "Internetworking Considerations."** Chapter 2 discusses the options available for placing your Web server on the Internet and making the Web sites housed on it available to clients. This chapter also includes a survey of third-party hardware and software solutions for guaranteeing the availability of your Web sites.

- **Chapter 3: "Integrating IIS with Windows 2000 Security."** Chapter 3 is the first of two security chapters in this book. This chapter first introduces the security measures available to Internet Information Services and then reviews the options provided by Windows 2000, including users and groups; passwords, policies, and access tokens; NTFS; and authentication features.

- **Chapter 4: "IIS Security."** Chapter 4 supplements the first security chapter by discussing the security measures provided by Internet Information Services. This chapter discusses the role of IP address and domain name restrictions, access permissions, and user authentication in Internet Information Services 5.

- **Chapter 5: "Customizing WWW Sites."** Chapter 5 provides a technical discussion of HTTP clients and servers and discusses configuration options of a Web site, including virtual servers and virtual directories. It also discusses delegating administrative privileges and issues you'll deal with when working with local and remote directories.

- **Chapter 6: "Customizing the FTP Service."** Chapter 6 begins with a brief review of FTP architecture. This chapter then details options configured on the FTP Site tab, security accounts that can access an FTP site, and options configured on the Home Directory tab. Finally, this chapter provides a discussion of FTP virtual directories and a step-by-step setup of an FTP site.

- **Chapter 7: "Running Web Applications."** Chapter 7 overviews how to run Web applications on Internet Information Services. This chapter focuses on information needed by the Web server administrator, not a developer, and includes topics, such as MIME type configuration, ISAPI applications, and ASP applications.

- **Chapter 8: "Microsoft FrontPage Server Extensions."** Chapter 8 explains how to install and effectively configure the FrontPage2000 Server Extensions. This chapter then discusses administering the Server Extensions and configuring security. Finally, this chapter explains how FrontPage administrators connect to a FrontPage Web and how the Server Extensions integrate with other services.

- **Chapter 9: "SSL and Certificate Services."** Chapter 9 discusses Secure Sockets Layer and why it is fundamental to security, encryption, client certificate mapping, certificates, and certificate authorities. This chapter also provides a complete walk-through of the installation of Microsoft Certification Authority Server.

- **Chapter 10: "IIS SMTP Service and NNTP Service."** Chapter 10 overviews SMTP architecture, surveys SendMail components available for use with Internet Information Services, reviews the SMTP property sheets, and introduces NNTP.

- **Chapter 11: "Connecting to Databases."** Chapter 11 provides an architectural overview of Open Database Connectivity, details three methods of connecting to a database, outlines the pros and cons to using Microsoft SQL Server databases and Microsoft Access databases, and explains the concept of and need for version checking.

- **Chapter 12: "Managing Log Files."** Chapter 12 provides details of the different log file formats available in Internet Information Services 5 and discusses the benefits of each. It also surveys utilities that will interpret log file data and generate valuable statistics and reports. This chapter finishes with recommendations for managing log files.

- **Chapter 13: "Performance Tuning and Reliability."** Chapter 13 starts by discussing the Performance tab of the Web Site Properties sheet and the options available when configuring Web applications. This chapter then focuses on monitoring the performance of Internet Information Services and specific Web sites, improving the performance of Internet Information Services, and the effects of ASP pages on Internet Information Services.

Conventions Used in This Book

Use of the term *Internet Information Services* generally applies to Internet Information Services 5, although a large portion of the topics covered in this book also apply to Internet Information Server 4 and occasionally to versions earlier than that. If the information is new to Internet Information Services 5, I have tried to highlight that. If I felt that the information was not well-known but applied to multiple versions, I tried to highlight that also.

Following these same lines, *Windows 2000* generally applies to Windows 2000 Server. Internet Information Services is included in other flavors of Windows 2000, but my experience and testing is with Windows 2000 Server. Almost all the information on Windows 2000 is the same for all flavors, with the exception of the Professional version. Because Professional is targeted for the desktop, it does not offer all the features of Windows 2000 Server, and its Internet Information Services component does not offer all the features of the Internet Information Services component included with Windows 2000 Server.

In addition, there are also a few typographical conventions in the book. Anything the reader selects or types is set off with bold; check boxes are in quotes; and Web sites, filenames, and utilities are monospaced font.

Installing and Managing IIS

THINKING ABOUT CONTENT AND THE BEST ways to organize content on your Internet Information Services server before you start implementation can save a lot of time and energy. This chapter covers key information that will make your installation and initial configuration smooth and successful.

Topics covered in this chapter include the following:

- Questions to consider before installing Internet Information Services
- Requirements of and recommendations for hardware and software needed to install IIS
- A short discussion of security planning
- Recommendations for organizing content and directory structures during installation
- Specific recommendations when installing Windows 2000 and IIS for a dedicated Web server
- Methods for managing IIS
- Backup options for your vital content

Before Installation

Think through the following questions before installing and deploying Internet Information Services 5:

- Will this Web server be placed behind a firewall?
- How much traffic do I expect, and have I provisioned all the necessary bandwidth?
- What type of content am I deploying? Is it active or dynamic, and will it access a database?
- Will Web users need to write or modify data on the server?
- Have I provisioned an adequate hardware configuration for my Web site utilization?
- Do I have the resources to manage this Internet Information Server computer if it becomes hugely successful?
- What security do I need for the physical server?
- Do I have plans for security, backups, and fault tolerance?
- Will this Windows 2000 server participate in a Windows domain?
- Will the Web server host one Web site or multiple Web sites?

When you can answer these questions, you are ready to plan the installation.

System Requirements

Internet Information Services 5 must be installed on a Windows 2000 server. It is not backward-compatible, so it cannot be installed on a Windows NT 4 server—or any other operating system, for that matter. By default, Internet Information Services 5 is installed during the installation of a Windows 2000 server.

The first step in planning for an installation of Internet Information Services is provisioning adequate hardware and software resources. This section assists you in better understanding both the hardware and the software required to optimally deploy Internet Information Services 5.

Hardware

According to Microsoft, Internet Information Services requires the same hardware configuration as Windows 2000 Server software. Realistically, however, the hardware minimums for Windows 2000 probably aren't adequate hardware minimums either for Windows 2000 or for Internet Information Services, not to mention the additional Web applications you will probably install to energize your Web sites. This section goes beyond the minimum and recommended requirements, focusing on what I've found to be the most useful in building an Internet Information Services server. (My experience is with both Web servers hosting a single Web site and Web servers hosting up to 50 Web sites.)

The following list discusses my recommendations for each hardware component:

- **Processor.** Look for at least a Pentium III 350MHz or better. If you can justify the minor cost increase, I recommend that you configure a dual processor server. Xeon processors can also boot the performance of your Web server because of their larger cache.

- **Memory.** Use at least 256MB of RAM, even if you are deploying only Windows 2000 without Internet Information Services. Actually, the preferred amount of RAM is at least 512MB, because memory is an inexpensive way of reducing latency and increasing the overall performance of Internet Information Services.

- **Hard drives.** Deploy at least two hard drives in an Internet Information Services server. The first drive is the system drive; the second is a data drive. This is also a good system strategy for security purposes, and increases the chance of recovery, should the system drive fail. Deploy SCSI-based drive technology with high RPM and low latency. Of course, the larger the drive, the better when allowing for future growth.

- **RAID.** A RAID 5 (redundant array of inexpensive disks) array is basically a collection of drives treated as one drive but divided into one or more partitions. RAID is recommended for any server that will require nonstop operations and that cannot tolerate data loss or drive failure which forces the server to go offline. More commonly known as *disk mirroring*, RAID 5 requires two hard drives: one configured as a regular drive, and the second to provide an exact copy of structure of the first in real time. Disk mirroring is a simple and inexpensive way to guarantee against data loss, and is configurable in Windows 2000 without additional software.

- **Network interface card (NIC).** Because IIS is network-intensive by nature, consider your network card an investment and buy PCI NICs that support 100Mbps connections. If you have only a 10Mbps connection today, buy a NIC that supports both 10Mbps and 100Mbps to support future network enhancements. Also, make sure you're buying a good name-brand NIC, such as 3COM or Intel.

- **Video.** A video card and monitor are required to install Windows 2000, but many Web servers do not have monitors connected to them when they are live on the network. Generally, SVGA monitors allow for better refresh rates and proper display of color when viewing your Web site locally. You will probably also find that an 800 × 600 display with at least 256 colors works best for pcANYWHERE and many other third-party software screens.

- **Mass media devices.** Of course, you will need a CD-ROM for most software installations. You may also need a backup solution. I like to install IOMEGA JAZZ drives in my Web servers for smaller backups.

At our company, ConnectOS Corporation, we have recently implemented a new backup device called an Onstream ADR tape drive. We have found this drive to be very useful and versatile, working first with Windows NT 4.0 Backup and then moving to Veritas Backup Exec software. Dollar for dollar, the Onstream drive provides the most storage space for the least expensive price.

Additional Hardware Considerations

Today, you can purchase inexpensive systems with very large IDE hard drives. These systems are ideal for general-purpose workstations or desktops, but the IDE drives cannot provide the sustained high output that can be achieved with SCSI (Small Computer System Interface) drives. SCSI is distributed with multiple interfaces, including Wide and Ultra Wide (which currently provides the best drive performance). Another benefit of SCSI is its bus-mastering capability, which means that the SCSI controller processes I/O requests instead of the system CPU. A good SCSI card will also include an I/O cache. You should use a SCSI controller that is built into the system motherboard or the SCSI controller that is a part of any RAID 5 controller, or purchase a name-brand controller, such as an Adaptec card.

Fault protection and the capability to recover data in the event of a failure can affect whether you are in business tomorrow. If you run a Web server at all times and a hard disk crashes, you will most likely experience unacceptable downtime, even with properly maintained backups. Naturally, downtime equals revenue loss and possibly the loss of clients. The most cost-effective way of reduce this type of downtime is to operate your Web servers in a data redundant mode—that is, make use of RAID technology. Several levels of RAID exist, but RAID 5 (also called RAID Level 5) is the optimal level.

When deciding between hardware and software RAID, keep in mind that hardware RAID provides the best performance, although software RAID is less expensive. The performance penalty of a software RAID solution will affect your Web server considerably in a high-demand environment. The bottom line is that a SCSI RAID 5 array will enable you to immediately recover from a failed hard drive and schedule its replacement at a more appropriate time.

Optimal Hard Drive Configuration

I see three separate disk requirements on my Web server: system files, log files, and Web data. With two hard drives of a minimum size of 10GB, I mirror a system partition, usually labeled as C:, and a log file partition, usually labeled E:. That provides 2GB to 4GB of system storage and 6GB to 8GB of log file storage, depending on the specific server. Then, I use three hard drives in a RAID 5 configuration with a SCSI RAID controller for Web data storage, and optionally a fourth hard drive for data regeneration in case one drive fails. This provides at least 10GB of Web data storage and fault tolerance.

Clustering multiple servers provides another fault-tolerant option. This topic is covered in the Chapter 2, "Internetworking Considerations."

Software

Successfully deploying Internet Information Services 5 requires only two software components: Windows 2000 with the Internet Information Services component and TCP/IP networking, and Internet Explorer 5.0 or later.

Internet Information Services 5 can be installed on either Windows 2000 Server or Windows 2000 Professional. I use Windows 2000 Server for my production Web servers. Windows 2000 Professional is most commonly used for development servers.

Security Preview

As an integrated service of Windows 2000, Internet Information Services takes full advantage of Windows 2000 security. Directories, files, scripts, and applications can all be made available for anonymous access over the Web or can be secured to particular users and groups.

Planning the security of your Web server is something to which you should devote considerable time. Because of the countless security options, both in Windows 2000 and in Internet Information Services, most of the security information in this book is contained in two chapters: Chapter 3, "Integrating IIS with Windows 2000 Security," and Chapter 4, "IIS Security." Before installing Internet Information Services, you should review these chapters and consider the security configuration of your Web server.

The following list provides several preliminary security steps that you should take when installing Internet Information Services:

- **Remove Everyone permissions from all drives.** By default, Windows 2000 assigns the Everyone special group full permissions to every file and directory on the server. To reduce this potential security risk, instruct Windows 2000 to format the system partition with NTFS during installation of the operating system to allow Windows 2000 to configure proper security to the system files. After formatting any additional partitions with NTFS, remove the full permissions for the Everyone special group from all partitions.

- **Disable unnecessary Windows 2000 services.** The more services you have running on the Internet Information Services server, the more entry points you make available to process client requests. To better secure your server, remove these unnecessary entry points.

The following list outlines some of the services that are not required to successfully run Internet Information Services 5:

- Alerter
- ClipBook Server

- Computer Browser
- Messenger
- Spooler
- TCP/IP NetBIOS Helper

Organizing Content

When you've considered the system requirements, you're ready to plan the organization of your Web data. I can't stress enough how important content organization is. You must consider the physical location of your Web data and space allocation before you start to just populate the server with data.

Internet Information Services creates the following default directory structure on the partition you designate for data: `D:\INETPUB\`. . . . Under the INETPUB are directories for various features of Internet Information Services, such as the `. . .\WWWRoot` and `. . .\FTPRoot` directory. The `\WWWRoot` directory is the default location of all Web data.

To begin planning the content layout for your Web server, consider the following questions:

- **How many hard drives will I have, and how will they be configured?** The number and size of partitions available on your server determine the options and restrictions of your content configuration. If possible, you should segregate the operating system, Web data, and log files onto different drives or different partitions. In addition to providing simpler administration because of the organization, this may provide a performance increase, depending on the number and configuration of physical drives.

- **Will I need to support FrontPage Server Extensions?** FrontPage Server Extensions for multiple Virtual Servers on one physical server require that all home directories of the Virtual Servers be located at the same directory level as the . . . `\WWWRoot` directory—that is, within the `\InetPub` directory and not within the default location of the `\WWWRoot` directory.

- **Will I deploy more than one Virtual Server?** One Virtual Server is required for each Web site hosted on your Web server. Because most Internet Web sites are referenced by a domain name, the physical directory name for a Web site should be configured to match its domain name. For example, if you configure a Virtual Server that will be referenced on the Internet as `http://www.mediaevents.com`, you should configure the Virtual Server's home directory as `D:\InetPub\mediaevents.com\`. Note that `mediaevents.com` is a directory name, not a filename. This practice makes it easy to manage a large directory of Web sites.

Both Windows 2000 and Internet Information Services will make drive requests all the time. By installing a system drive and one or more separate data drives, you will reduce I/O bottlenecks, such as accessing a system file and a Web page at the same time. The system partition should be the partition to which all software is installed—that is, Windows 2000, third-party applications, and utilities. The data drive should consist of fault-tolerant drives containing the \InetPub directory and any other data, but not including log files.

Partitioning a single physical drive in multiple partitions does not provide the same performance improvements as installing two or more physical drives. You must use separate physical devices to take advantage of I/O improvements. Also, it may be of even more benefit to separate the drives onto different channels and to use multiple hard drive controllers.

Installation

Unlike Internet Information Server 4, Internet Information Services 5 installs as a component of the Windows 2000 Server operating system. Unless your environment requires you to upgrade from a previous version of Internet Information Server, you should freshly install Internet Information Services and Windows 2000 onto a newly formatted system. This will give you more control in customizing the system from a known state.

Windows 2000 Server will ask you multiple questions during installation to customize your system. One of these questions determines whether your Web server will exist within a Windows 2000 domain and, if so, whether it also will function as a domain controller. Whether your Web server is a member of a Windows 2000 domain depends on your network environment and your security requirements. If there is an existing domain that contains user accounts against which Web users may be validated, then you should certainly join the domain. The overhead for membership in a domain is minimal, and the administration of accounts is greatly simplified.

Because of both the processing and the network overhead of being a Windows 2000 domain controller, I almost always configure my Web servers as Member servers in the Windows 2000 domain. Whether or not your Web server is a domain controller, you can create local user accounts in Windows 2000 to secure your Web server and Web sites. However, one benefit to becoming a domain controller is that multiple Web servers can share the same local account database. The Microsoft domain model generates the same security account manager (SAM) database on all domain controllers. So, for example, if your environment includes three Web servers with Web sites that will be accessed by the same 10 Web administrators, you can either create 30 user accounts across three Web servers (which is not recommended by Microsoft because of the administration problems), or you can create 10 user accounts on one Web server and synchronize them across all three Web servers. Additional security information is provided in Chapters 3 and 4.

When installing Internet Information Services 5, you will probably need to choose a Custom installation, if for no other reason than to locate the \InetPub data directory on your designated data partition. Other than that, the default settings are generally acceptable, but you'll need to evaluate them individually for your environment.

The following Windows 2000 installation process highlights the installation options discussed so far in this chapter. During the installation of Windows 2000, take these steps:

1. During the installation of Windows 2000 Server, format the system partition with NTFS.

2. Locate Windows 2000 on the C: drive.

3. Optimize your swap file by setting it at 50% to 100% of your physical memory size. This should provide you with a page file between 128MB and 512MB.

4. Choose a Custom installation of Internet Information Services.

5. Locate the \InetPub directory on the data drive.

When the installation process is complete, continue modifying the server as follows:

1. Change boot timeout to 0 seconds.

2. Format or convert all remain partitions with NTFS.

3. Remove the Everyone special group from the drive permission lists.

Managing Internet Information Services

Internet Information Server 5 provides a several options for managing your Web server. This section briefly describes three of those options.

Microsoft Management Console

Beginning with Internet Information Server 4, Internet Information Services provides a snap-in to the Microsoft Management Console (MMC). The IIS snap-in replaces the Internet Server Manager that shipped with previous versions of Internet Information Server, although the Start menu program still reads Internet Server Manager.

The MMC is an extensible common console for managing network applications. The MMC itself provides no management capabilities; these features are implemented through incorporating snap-ins responsible for the management task. The console provides a common framework for managing these applications.

In the IIS snap-in, the scope pane (the left pane) is a tree displaying the tool's namespace. Each node in the tree represents a manageable object, task, or view. The scope pane may not be visible in all views. The result pane (the right pane) displays the result of selecting a node in the scope pane. As in Windows Explorer, the right pane often displays the contents of a folder or directory.

With MMC, you can create views with a combination of snap-ins from various programs and then save these views for later use or to share with other administrators. This approach enables you to efficiently create custom tools with different levels of complexity for delegating and coordinating tasks.

To start the MMC from the server with the Internet Information Services snap-in loaded, select *Internet Service Manager* from Start, Programs.

Browser-Based Administration

Also beginning with Internet Information Server 4, Microsoft began shipping a browser-based Internet Service Manager (ISM) that provides complete administrative control over the Web server, Web sites, and FTP sites. You can use the browser-based ISM to manage a Web server or to securely manage an individual Web site.

Although it is also possible to remotely manage a Web server using the browser-based ISM, the default restrictions deny access to all hosts except the local Web server. If you plan to use the browser-based ISM for remote management, you must first remove the IP address restrictions for the administrative Web site. I recommend that you modify these restrictions to allow access only to the locations from which you will manage your Web server to prevent unauthorized users from attempting to access your Web site remotely. For more information on IP address and domain name restrictions, see the section "IP Address and Domain Name Restrictions" in Chapter 4.

Remote Administration

It is also possible to administer an Internet Information Services server from a remote Windows 2000 server simply by installing the MMC and the appropriate snap-ins on the local system. To manage Internet Information Services, Microsoft Transaction Server, and most other programs remotely by using the MMC, you must have administrative privileges on the remote server. As with browser-based administration, be sure that you have secured the Web site from administration by unauthorized individuals. If you do not have appropriate permissions, you will receive an "Access Denied" error when connecting to the remote system.

Third-Party Options

Many third-party tools also are available for remotely administering both Windows 2000 and Internet Information Services.

One such tool, pcANYWHERE, by Symantec, enables you to fully view the Windows 2000 console screen and manage it as if you were sitting at the computer. It also includes a remote reboot feature and a separate file transfer utility.

If you plan to run a "lights-out" data center (that is, a data center that you rarely physically access and manage almost completely remotely), then pcANYWHERE is an excellent investment.

Backups

No matter what measures you take to reduce the chances of server failure, there will probably come a time when you will need to recover some amount of data for your Web server. In the case of a complete server failure, you must have data backups readily available.

Following are some backup strategies to consider:

- Create a backup plan that will, at a minimum, back up all the data on your Web server.

- Choose backup software that can run scheduled backups and provide simple restore procedures.

- Implement a backup schedule that will forfeit, at most, 24 hours' worth of data.

- Protect your backup media by storing it in a location other than that of your Web server.

- Maintain a fully stocked, easily accessible \Install directory that contains the files required for a full installation of a Web server, possibly including Windows 2000 plus all updated drivers, Internet Explorer, pcANYWHERE, and other third-party utilities.

Let me give an example of a full backup plan based on my environment. I procured one Windows 2000 server for the sole purpose of providing backups for my Web servers. In addition to having an Onstream 30GB ADR tape drive, this server is installed with Veritas Backup Exec software and contains my \Install directory on the data partition.

Each Sunday at 2:00 a.m. Pacific Time, a full backup is created automatically from multiple servers for all Web data, which is the \InetPub directory on each Web server. Then, at the same time on the remaining days of the week, an incremental backup automatically executes. Every four weeks, the backup tape is taken offsite and kept safe for one month, at which time it is reused.

The result of this plan is that it maintains two months' worth of backup data. In the best-case scenario, data can be recovered from a single tape that is already loaded in the backup server. In the worse case, we must reinstall a Web server across the LAN by using the \Install directory and restoring data from a backup tape that has been taken offsite. This takes much more time than the first scenario, and the restored data can be up to one month old. But either way, we can get a Web server or Web site back online quickly and with a minimal amount of effort.

Now that you have learned about the planning, installation, and administration options for Internet Information Services 5, you're ready to look at the details. Chapter 2 discusses internetworking. Chapter 3 and Chapter 4 deal with a topic relevant to both planning and administration: security. This starts with a review of Windows 2000 security and its synergy with Internet Information Services security. Immediately following that is a close look at each of the security features of Internet Information Services 5.

2

Internetworking Considerations

INTERNET INFORMATION SERVICES CAN BE configured in either an intranet or an Internet environment. In either environment, IIS is installed on a Windows 2000 server, and the server is connected to a network and running the TCP/IP protocol. This illustrates that the primary difference between an intranet and the Internet is simply that one environment is bigger than the other—a lot bigger.

But because the Internet is such a large environment, considerable options are available to make IIS function optimally on it. This chapter should provide an administrator with the full breadth of products and technologies that might be needed to successfully implement an IIS solution. Much of this information relates to third-party products and other products not generally associated with IIS. This chapter also covers some Internet solutions, such as DNS round-robin, which can further assist in providing a well-rounded solution.

Specifically, this chapter covers the following topics:

- A discussion of Web hosting options, including shared servers, co-located servers, dedicated servers, and data centers
- An overview of domains and domain registrations, with a case study of DNS Round Robin
- A survey of hardware and software solutions for guaranteeing the availability of Internet Information Services sites
- A discussion of how to create exact replicas of data to support a fault-tolerant environment

Hosting Options

Although the Internet has come to be known as a "virtual" entity, it is important to understand the implications of informed decisions regarding the hardware and physical attributes of your Internet site. The right decision is a balance between the amount of control you can maintain over your site and the cost of hosting it. These costs can include leveraging fault-tolerance solutions and bandwidth aggregation. Good planning will also enable you to grow your site later with little complication.

The four basic types of Web site hosting options are a shared server, a dedicated server, a co-located server, and a data center location. Of course, you always have the option of hosting your own Web server. The same issues defined in the following sections should apply to the decision to take your Internet Information Services server in-house.

Shared Server

Today's new innovative and modern computers enable you to distribute the processing capability and storage capacity of a single computer among multiple Web sites. The computer hosting the multiple Web sites is called a *shared server*. With the flexibility of Microsoft Internet Information Services and a relatively powerful computer, you could literally host thousands of Web sites on a single computer. The number and scope of these sites, of course, is limited by the speed and storage capacity of the system and the bandwidth of the connection to the Internet. A single Web site on a shared server is referred to as a *virtual server* because it appears as a single Web site on a single computer.

In addition to a generally lower cost, a Web site on a shared server provides the benefit of less administrative management. A Web site owner can control the Web site's content without knowing how to manage IIS or even Microsoft Windows 2000.

However, the overall performance of any Web site on a server will depend to some extent not only on its own content and usage, but also on the content and usage of any other sites residing on the same computer. For small- to medium-sized sites that contain primarily static content, a shared server is often a good value. This generally is recommended as a starting point, allowing for cost savings during the learning period that should determine what you really want a Web site to do and, thus, what it will require.

When selecting a hosting company with a shared server environment, consider some of the following issues:

- How many Web sites are hosted on a single server?
- Do you have access to the log files for your Web site?
- Will the company support Secure Sockets Layer (SSL)?
- Can you use an Access database or SQL database if needed?
- What if you outgrow the shared servers?
- What happens if your site stops functioning as 3:00 a.m.?
- What kind of support is available to you?

These are just a few of the questions to consider when you define your requirements. You might want to test the performance of other Web sites hosted on the company's shared servers and run a TRACERT to verify the Internet connectivity. Hundreds of companies offer these services, so take the time to pick the one that's right for your Web site.

Co-location and Dedicated Servers

When you need almost total control over your own Web site, you may use a co-location or a dedicated server, which many Internet providers offer. The term *dedicated server* implies that the Internet provider owns the server, both the hardware and the software. The term *co-location server* implies that you own the server.

Also, keep in mind that the growth of a Web site's size and popularity will inevitably affect the overall "fitness" of the site. When a site has outgrown a shared server, either in size or in consumption of resources, it may be necessary for the site to be moved to a server of its own.

With a dedicated server, the specifications of hardware and software are usually determined by the Internet provider. However, when you own the equipment in a co-location, you have control over which hardware is used and which software is installed and run on the system. You also control other factors, such as security, config-uration, and maintenance of the site—usually resulting in a lower cost from the Internet provider. On the other hand, support from the Internet provider for co-loca-tion equipment is minimal, and the technical expertise necessary to run the server will be higher for you, the client.

Co-location servers and dedicated servers are similar from a logistical stance. Both servers usually contain a single Web site residing on a single computer, but this is not always the case. You will likely receive administrative access to the server, at least remotely, and share in the responsibility of its management. You may or may not have the capability to host multiple sites on the server, or in effect create your own shared server. Other important considerations are the tools and applications available from the ISP. You might need your own server to load additional software not provided or supported by the ISP.

One benefit of a co-location or dedicated server is that it allows your Web site to be placed directly on a high-speed network connected directly to the Internet without the significant cost of a dedicated high-speed connection. For example, if you have a high-traffic Web site and want to provide 45Mbps of bandwidth to the server, you could get your own T3 Internet connection for tens of thousands of dollars per month, or you could get a co-location or dedicated server connected to your Internet provider's high-speed connection for a fraction of the cost.

Data Centers

When your services have outgrown co-location or dedicated servers, either one or many, it's time to evaluate your own data center. Although many options are available, the most effective choice is to contact an Internet backbone provider that has a large data center and rent a full *rack* or a *cage*. In addition to a warehouse-style location, a data center typically provides amenities, such as redundant power, fire suppression, and physical security.

A cage is exactly that: a fenced-in area of about 50 to 75 square feet with a locking gate. A cage usually contains up to five racks, or cabinets. A rack holds up to six servers, depending on the size of the computers and peripheral computers. The benefits to a cage include a reduction in space costs per server and better access to your hardware.

If you choose to acquire a cage, you will also need to get an allocation of bandwidth. Bandwidth is usually charged separately and depends entirely on the level you want. In this case, you are paying your Internet backbone provider for a portion of its connection to the Internet. For example, you could opt to pay for 1Mbps of bandwidth whether you use it all or not, and thus pay a flat discounted price. Or, you could choose to pay for a base, or minimum, of 10Mbps with the ability to burst into 100Mbps, and pay a bit higher rate per megabits per second used. Either way, the cost is a lot less than buying your own dedicated connection.

DNS Configuration

Another crucial consideration of internetworking is host name configuration. Although users can enter the IP address of a Web site into their Web browser, it is much simpler if they can type a common name. This common name is typically defined by a host name and a domain name, which are together called a fully qualified domain name (FQDN). To allow Web users to type an FQDN into their Web browsers, you need to register a domain name on the Internet and assign it an IP address on the computer running Internet Information Services.

For example, when I wanted to create a Web site called www.youngcountry.net, I registered youngcountry.net using a domain registration service (see the next section, "Domain Registration"). I then assigned it an IP address and mapped it to www.youngcountry.net by using a domain name server (DNS). Then, I configured the DNS servers with a zone file named youngcountry.net.dns. Within this zone file, the IP address assigned to the Web site is associated with a resource record for youngcountry.net and www.

Following is the zone file of youngcountry.net.dns:

```
@    IN    SOA    ns1.connectos.net.    dnsadmin.connectos.net.    (
     2              ; serial number
     3600           ; refresh
     600            ; retry
     86400          ; expire
     3600        )  ; minimum TTL
@    IN    NS     ns1.connectos.net.
@    IN    NS     ns2.connectos.net.
@    IN    A      10.10.50.100
```

When a user types `http://www.youngcountry.net` into a browser,
`www.youngcountry.net` is resolved to the assigned IP address. The routers on the
Internet then find the server configured with the IP address, and Internet Information
Services sends the user the correct Web page.

All information related to a domain, including the authoritative DNS servers, the
name and address of the owner, and the administrative contact, is stored in a public
database available on the Internet. Figure 2.1 displays a sample of this information that
was queried by using a Whois query.

Domain Registration

When you register your domain name, you will be required to specify the IP address
of at least two DNS servers. The top level domain (TLD) servers will associate your
domain name with the DNS servers designated. For example, when our company
registered the domain `youngcountry.net`, the `.net` DNS servers were configured to
point to our DNS servers downstream. The root DNS servers (".") were already
configured to point all `.net` inquiries to the `.net` DNS servers.

Today, there are many more TLDs than there were just a few years ago. As `.com`
domain suffixes were scooped up, `.net`, `.org`, `.to`, and others became more visible.
Still, the most common domain suffixes need to be registered with Network
Solutions. To register a domain name or find out the requirements of doing so, look
at `http://www.networksolutions.com`.

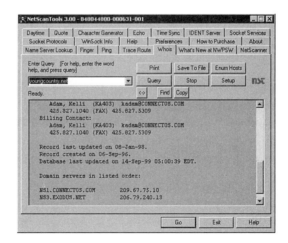

Figure 2.1   A Whois query using NetScanTools lists
the domain registrant and DNS information.

Domains and Subdomains

You can also configure subdomains in DNS. Suppose that our company's corporate servers were all in the `corp.connectos.com` domain. The root DNS servers would point to the `.com` DNS servers, which would point to the `connectos.com` DNS servers, which would then point to the `corp.connectos.com` DNS server. In our case, both `connectos.com` and `corp.connectos.com` would all be the same physical servers, but would always require unique DNS configuration files, also called *zone* files. After we configure these subdomains, we can create servers, such as `research1.corp.connectos.com` and `hr1.corp.connectos.com`.

A subdomain does not appear to be as simple as a standard domain name. However, there are several benefits to using a subdomain. First, there is no charge from an Internet domain registrar because subdomains are provided by the domain owner. Secondly, any modifications to subdomains are immediate because changes are made only to the primary DNS server.

Although a wide variety of reasons exist for using a domain name, Internet Information Services generally does not require the use of domain names. In an intranet, the service could be accessed by the computer name, and in either an intranet or the Internet, the service could be accessed by an IP address. It's not pretty, but it works. The only time that Internet Information Services 5 requires the use of a domain name is when a host header is configured. This issue is addressed later in Chapter 5, "Customizing WWW Sites."

DNS Round Robin

Another option for domain configuration is DNS Round Robin, which is the simplest and most cost-effective way to emulate load balancing. This method does not provide any true load-balancing features for server traffic; instead, it simply distributes connections between one or more Web servers as they are received.

To implement DNS Round Robin, create multiple resource records within a zone file. Each record will use the same host name but a different IP address on a different server for each Web site. To set up DNS Round Robin for two servers, do the following:

1. Make an exact copy of the Web site files and directories on two or more Web servers.

2. Create a WWW virtual server on each Web server. Configure each virtual server to use the local files copied in step 1. Configure each virtual server with a unique IP address.

3. Test each Web site by using the IP address to be sure each Web site functions the same way.

4. Create a resource record, commonly called an A record, in DNS for the Web site that resolves to the first IP address.

5. Create an additional resource record, or an A record, for each IP address assigned in step 2. The host name must be the same, but the IP address must be different.

For example, suppose you have a high-traffic Web site that you want to be distributed across three servers. Create a subdirectory called `website.com` on the server named `Webhost1` in the `\InetPub` directory, and copy the content of the Web site into the directory structure. Repeat the procedure for `Webhost2` and `Webhost3`, respectively. On `Webhost1`, create a WWW virtual server by using a valid local IP address—for example, 10.50.50.100. Do the same for `Webhost2` and `Webhost3`, respectively. For example, you could use the IP address 10.50.25.100 for `Webhost2`, and 10.50.75.100 for `Webhost3`. Test each Web site by using its IP address.

To configure the DNS Round Robin, create a resource record for WWW in the `website.com` zone file that points to the IP address of the virtual server on `Webhost1`. Then, create a second resource record for WWW in the `website.com` zone file that points to the IP address of the virtual server on `Webhost2`. The following is the text version of the `website.com` zone file:

```
@     IN     SOA     ns1.website.com.     dnsadmin.website.com.     (
      2                ; serial number
      3600             ; refresh
      600              ; retry
      86400            ; expire
      3600          )  ; minimum TTL
@     IN     NS      ns1.website.com.
www   IN     A       10.50.50.100
www   IN     A       10.50.25.100
www   IN     A       10.50.75.100
```

When a user connects to `http://www.website.com` from a Web browser, the DNS server will respond as follows:

1. Returns `10.50.50.100` in response to the first request
2. Returns `10.50.25.100` in response to the second request
3. Returns `10.50.75.100` in response to the third request
4. Begins again with responses from the top of the list, then returns `10.50.50.100` in response to the fourth request, and so on

Problems with DNS Round Robin

DNS Round Robin does not provide true load balancing or fault tolerance because DNS does not verify the resources on any servers before resolving the name to IP address. So, if a significant number of users disconnect from a single server when using DNS Round Robin, new connections would still be distributed evenly across all servers. Thus, some servers would maintain more connections than others.

Also, other DNS servers will cache the DNS information and simply return it to new clients without checking again with the authoritative DNS server. For example, it is likely that all employees at a large company have the same DNS servers configured. When the first user from this company connects to a Web site, the DNS resolution will be cached by the local DNS server. If a large number of users continues to connect to that same Web site from this company, they will all be given the cached DNS information.

Handling Capacity Requirements

The exponential growth of the Internet has created significant challenges for Web administrators, including the following:

- Verifying the constant availability of WWW and FTP services
- Distributing Internet services across globally dispersed data centers
- Maximizing performance of Internet services
- Reducing costs associated with providing distributed Internet services
- Redirecting client traffic away from offline servers to online servers

The conventional solution to resolving capacity requirements has been simply to replace an existing server with a bigger and faster model or to add server capacity. However, multiple hardware and software solutions provide a more cost-effective and advantageous approach. The following sections give examples of solutions you can use to load balance, handle fault tolerance, provide content replication, and so on, through various hardware and software solutions.

System Monitoring

The basic premise behind capacity planning is to guarantee the constant availability of your WWW and FTP services. But, regardless of whether or not you employ any of the solutions described later in this chapter, you need a way to verify that availability.

I first realized that I needed real-time network monitoring when a colleague of mine glanced at his pager for the second time during lunch one day and casually announced, "I love knowing that my Web server can recover without my assistance in less than five minutes." His first page was an automatic notice that his Web server had failed. His second page was an automatic notice that the server was again available. I will not go into detail at this point about scripts and reboots, but you get the point. I told him that I needed this type of solution. Now, I can't image how I ever slept at night without it.

When I first implemented a system-monitoring tool, WhatsUp Gold, by Ipswitch, Inc., was the best choice, but it also was really the only choice. Later, MediaHouse Software, Inc., produced Enterprise Monitor 5.0. Both products effectively verify the availability of system services.

I recommend installing a system-monitoring tool on a separate server from your Web servers. It doesn't do any good to have a monitoring tool in place if the server the monitoring tool is installed on is the same server that the monitoring tool needs to monitor, and it all fails. To configure a monitoring tool most effectively, you need to install it on two servers: one to monitor all your servers, and one to monitor the first installation of the monitoring tool. Now, every server is being monitored, including the two monitoring servers.

WhatsUp Gold by Ipswitch, Inc.

WhatsUp Gold has a graphical interface that uses color to indicate the status of the protocols on each server. It can monitor multiple protocols, including HTTP, FTP, SNMP, and POP3. If any service doesn't respond in a user-defined amount of time, it can send emails or LAN notifications. I have it configured to send email to support staff, and a pager notification via email to the system administrator.

WhatsUp Gold is easy to install and simple to use. It also supports other protocols, including IPX/SPX and NetBEUI. As a nice bonus, it includes a collection of TCP/IP utilities, such as Lookup, Whois, and Finger.

Ipswitch also produces a non-Gold version of WhatsUp. Some of the features available only in the Gold version make it the mandatory choice for Internet Information Services administrators. First, the Gold version installs as a Windows 2000 service, allowing you to log off the server without shutting off the monitoring. Secondly, it provides Web-based administration so that you can easily manage it from any client with a Web browser.

My only issue with WhatsUp Gold is the timeout options. One of our company's clients had a Web site that would slow down to a crawl every morning. The good news is that they were working on putting a more robust server in place. But the bad news is that my system administrator received a page every morning at 6:30 a.m. stating that the server was down. She knew it was just a timeout, not a true down situation, but we couldn't get WhatsUp Gold to wait long enough to realize that the site really was available.

Enterprise Monitor by MediaHouse Software, Inc.

MediaHouse Software, Inc., has been producing BBS-related utilities for years. When the Web began to erode their market, however, they moved to Web server tools specifically designed for Microsoft servers. The company's flagship product is Statistics Server, which is covered later in Chapter 12, "Managing Log Files."

Enterprise Monitor provides similar functionality as WhatsUp Gold for about half the price. It installs as a Windows 2000 service and polls services or devices for availability. It boasts the ease of Web-based administration and the capability to locate devices on the network. But I find its best features to be its support for dependencies and its capability to run batch files as a recovery option.

Dependencies enable you to set up a hierarchy of required services. When configuring dependencies, for example, you could indicate that a specific Web site is dependent on its SQL server database. If the SQL server fails, then of course the Web site won't return the expected response. But instead of receiving a down notification for both the SQL server and then the Web site, you would receive only one notification for the failed SQL server.

The other exciting feature of Enterprise Monitor is its capability to run batch files through its Recovery Script option. Two of the batch files that ship with the product allow an automatic restart of a failed service or an automatic reboot of a failed server. You can also create your own batch files and run third-party applications.

Although the basic functionality of Enterprise Monitor is similar to that of WhatsUp, it has more options and costs less. I still find that more administrators are familiar with WhatsUp, but other options are available.

Load Balancing

Load balancing is the efficient distribution of Internet services among globally dispersed Internet server sites. Different methods for achieving this include the use of the intelligence built into Internet routing to divert traffic from a failed route, standard domain name service (DNS) services configured in a round-robin fashion, and the Hypertext Transfer Protocol (HTTP).

Most load-balancing products redirect Internet traffic to multiple servers based on current server capacity, service requested, speed of server services, or source address. Servers and services can easily be added, removed, or reallocated depending on traffic demands and patterns. These load-balancing products have the capability to maintain a consistent number of connections between multiple servers. If a significant number of users disconnect from a single server, new connections would be routed to the server with the fewest possible connections until the load was balanced once again.

By distributing user requests across a cluster of servers, load-balancing products optimize server responsiveness and system capacity and dramatically reduce the cost of providing mission-critical services. Additionally, load-balancing products provide fault tolerance by assuring the continuous, high availability of services.

The typical load-balancing products support management via Simple Network Management Protocol (SNMP). SNMP can be used to report traffic data for Web servers and availability of services. Many load-balancing products also support administrative notifications via logs or email at preconfigured thresholds.

Fault Tolerance

Another approach to handling capacity requirements is fault tolerance. As you may know, *fault tolerance* is a generic term for the guarantee of resource availability even in the event of a serious problem. For example, suppose that you own two cars but only drive one to and from work each day. Then, one day you find that the engine doesn't start on the car you drive to work. You still get to work, probably even on time, because you can take the second car. No one ever knows the difference. You have a fault-tolerant transportation system.

Most load-balancing solutions inherently support fault tolerance of the servers they are load balancing. If you have multiple servers to which you can distribute service requests, then you obviously have contingent services in place in case one server fails. All you need to do is take the failed server out of the pool of accessible servers.

However, because a load-balancing solution is, in itself, a server of some sort, you need to plan for fault tolerance of the load balancer. The optimal solution is to configure two load balancers that are aware of each other.

Fault tolerance as described here is also sometimes referred to as *fault-tolerant clustering*. *Clustering* is the configuration of multiple servers that perform the same tasks. However, the configuration of the cluster can provide full or only partial fault tolerance. Microsoft Cluster Server is discussed later in this chapter, but the concept behind it is relevant to fault tolerance solutions.

Hardware Solutions

The two predominant hardware solutions for both load balancing and fault tolerance for Internet services are Cisco's LocalDirector and DistributedDirector, and F5 Lab's BIG/ip and 3DNS. Both LocalDirector and BIG/ip are positioned for a single data center, while both DistributedDirector and 3DNS are positioned for multiple geographically dispersed data centers. Figure 2.2 diagrams the configuration required for either fault tolerance or load balancing.

Keep in mind, though, that to provide true fault tolerance, you need to implement two of the servers discussed here. Otherwise, you have created a single point of failure with this solution.

Cisco LocalDirector and DistributedDirector

Cisco LocalDirector tracks network sessions and server load conditions in real time, directing each session to the most appropriate server. All physical servers together

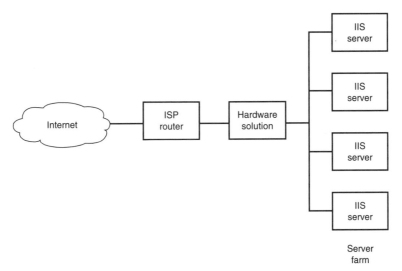

Figure 2.2   Fault tolerance and load balancing require that multiple Web servers be accessible to the hardware solution.

appear as one virtual server, with the result that only a single IP address and a single uniform resource locator (URL) are required for an entire server farm.

LocalDirector also allows for graceful shutdown of servers and automatic slow start of servers recently brought back into service. For geographically dispersed servers, LocalDirector can work in conjunction with DistributedDirector to direct user traffic to the nearest available server. DistributedDirector provides load distribution among multiple geographically dispersed servers. DistributedDirector utilizes Cisco Internetwork Operating System (Cisco IOS™) software and leverages routing table information in the network infrastructure to transparently redirect end-user service requests to the geographically nearest responsive server.

Cisco LocalDirector 410 is priced at approximately $30,000. Cisco DistributedDirector is priced at about half that (installation and service are extra). Although the Cisco solutions provide exactly what they intend to provide, I like the more comprehensive solution provided by F5 Labs.

F5 Labs BIG/ip and 3DNS

BIG/ip from F5 Labs is a comprehensive solution for Internet hosting providers. Using seven different metrics, it provides excellent load balancing and fault tolerance. It can also provide notification of failed systems or services, Windows 2000 Event logging, real-time performance monitoring, and rate shaping. Because it functions as an IP router, it also can provide firewall services.

BIG/ip appears to be the solution of choice for many Internet companies. Over the past two years, the number of BIG/ip servers located at a data center in Seattle have increased almost 10 times—and after hearing a presentation from F5 Labs, I can see why. The product is comprehensive, and the company's sales force knows it well.

The price for BIG/ip is about the same as that of Cisco's LocalDirector. However, in this case, the price includes an unlimited server license, two days of onsite installation, and a full service plan.

Software Solutions

Three software solutions provide at least partial fault-tolerance for Internet services: Loadbal, Microsoft Cluster Server, and Windows 2000's TCP/IP Network Load Balancing. The following sections examine these in greater detail.

Loadbal

Loadbal is an ActiveX component that ships with the Internet Information Server 4 Resource Kit. It constantly monitors Performance Monitor data on the clustered servers to determine which is experiencing the lowest load and then directs traffic to that server. For more information on the Loadbal solution, see the Microsoft Internet Information Services Resource Kit.

Microsoft Cluster Server

Windows 2000 Advanced Server includes a product called Microsoft Cluster Server (previously code-named "Wolfpack") that provides partial fault tolerance. Microsoft Cluster Server software is installed on two identically configured Internet Information Services servers. Both servers, though, are connected to a single, shared SCSI drive array or a Fiber Channel array. If one server fails, the other detects the failure and takes over all services. However, if you lose power to the drive array, for example, all services fail. When using Microsoft Cluster Server, you should definitely configure the drives for RAID 5.

TCP/IP Network Load Balancing (NLB)

Originally developed as Convoy Cluster software and previously known as Windows Load Balancing Service in Windows NT 4, Network Load Balancing (NLB) is a feature of Windows 2000 Advanced Server that enables organizations to load balance among up to 32 servers running Windows 2000 Advanced Server. This allows NLB to evenly distribute network traffic to multiple servers. When a computer fails or goes offline for maintenance, NLB automatically reconfigures the cluster to direct client requests to functioning servers, thereby maintaining continuous availability of network services. NLB is an excellent solution for load balancing full servers configured with one IP address each. But a shared Internet Information Services server may have multiple IP addresses configured to support multiple Web sites. In this case, NLB enables you to configure load balancing to each site individually by using its configured IP address.

When NLB is started, it invokes a convergence process in which each server broadcasts its status to the other server(s) in the cluster. The servers all agree on the current state of the cluster and begin load balancing based on the consensus of the convergence process. When additional computers are added, the convergence state is updated, and service continues. If one of the computers in the cluster fails, the convergence state is again immediately updated and the failed server is effectively removed from the cluster by the other servers.

Content Replication

When distributing requests among multiple servers, keep in mind the importance of ensuring that the content of your servers is *mirrored*, or copied identically, across all the servers. When a Web page on one server is updated, for example, all the servers that contain the same Web page should be updated at the same time. *Content replication* means that data on multiple servers is synchronized or mirrored to be an exact replica of the other servers. While periodically backing up the default server to the other servers may be suitable for some Web sites, the most efficient and effective method requires an automatic real-time service to instantly update all the content on your clustered Web site.

Windows 2000 Replication Service

One option to ensure content replication is the Windows 2000 Replication service. It enables you to quickly, easily, and cheaply (it's free) replicate content from one server to another. To use the Windows 2000 Replication service, configure one computer in a cluster to receive all content updates. Then, configure that computer as an export server, specifying that the directory structure is available for download. Next, configure all other computers in the cluster as import servers, and point to the directory on the export server for the source data.

When content is updated on the export server, that server notifies the import servers of the data change, and the import servers request and receive the new content. All servers will almost immediately be exact replicas of one another. In the case of any server failing, including the export server, fault tolerance will keep the Web site available, and content replication will guarantee that the data is current.

The main drawback to the Windows 2000 Replication service is that is a very basic application. It only copies information to the other servers; it doesn't provide a way to configure the services or even to copy the configuration from one Web site to another.

Microsoft Content Replication System

Another option is the Microsoft Content Replication System (CRS) feature of Microsoft Site Server. It also duplicates information across Web servers, although the replication can be scheduled. This may not work in your scenario if you need to be sure that all servers contain identical content at all times. However, in some scenarios it is an excellent option. For example, suppose that a company uses a staging server for content deployment. During the day, updates are made to the staging server and are tested. By the end of the day, the Web site has been updated to a new, existing version. Microsoft CRS can be configured to replicate the staging server to the live server or servers every night at midnight.

Although Microsoft CRS is a great solution for content deployment, it alone cannot justify the cost of Microsoft Site Server. For a list of the other features of Site Server or Microsoft Commercial Internet System (MCIS), see the Microsoft Web site, www.microsoft.com.

Now that you've learned about the planning, installation, and integration of Internet Information Services, you're ready to begin configuring the Web server. The next two chapters discuss its security configuration, which has been divided into Windows 2000 security measures and Internet Information Services security measures.

3

Integrating IIS with Windows 2000 Security

W INDOWS 2000 SECURITY IS THE SECURITY model upon which Internet
Information Services security rests. Securing an Internet Information Services server
requires a combination of both Internet Information Services and Windows 2000
security measures. Before covering the security features of IIS in the next
chapter, it is necessary to discuss Windows 2000 security.

This chapter covers the following topics:

- How Windows 2000 security works with Internet Information Services
- How Windows 2000 users and groups interact with Internet Information
  Services, including passwords, policies, and access tokens
- How to optimize security with NTFS
- How to take advantage of the auditing and logging features of Internet
  Information Services

How Windows 2000 Security Works with IIS

Windows 2000 security protects your computer and its resources by requiring user
accounts for all operations. You can control access to all computer resources, including
Web content, by limiting the user rights of these accounts. Windows 2000 maintains
account lists of local users and groups, and of users and groups within a domain.

Internet Information Services utilizes a four-step process in controlling Web site access. When IIS receives a request to access a site, it first checks for specific IP address restrictions. Next, it verifies the user account. The third step for the server is to verify Web site permissions. Finally, IIS checks NTFS permissions to control access to folders and files. Of these steps, the last step is a Windows 2000 security feature discussed in this chapter. Although the other three are security features of IIS, the second step, which verifies the user, works in conjunction with Windows 2000. Because of this tight relationship, this chapter also introduces user and group accounts. Finally, the chapter looks at some additional Windows 2000 security recommendations, as well as auditing and logging. The next chapter focuses on security features of Internet Information Services. Figure 3.1 shows a graphical representation of the IIS security process.[1]

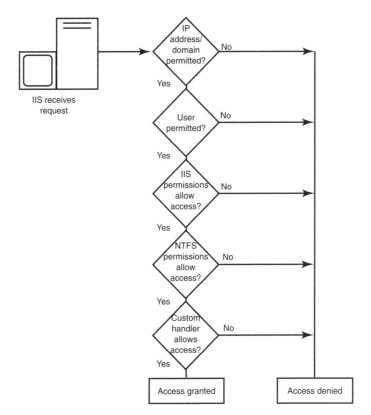

Figure 3.1   Internet Information Services uses a
five-step process to control Web site access.

[1] Note that in Figure 3.1, there are five steps instead of four. In addition to the standard steps, IIS gives you the flexibility of creating your own custom security handler.

Windows 2000 Security Recommendations

Before Internet Information Services ever enters the picture, Windows 2000 will have been installed and configured on your computer. To fully secure Internet Information Services, you must first secure the underlying foundation, Microsoft Windows 2000. The following list is just the beginning of the measures that you can take to secure Microsoft Windows 2000:

- Remove unnecessary protocols, such as NWLink IPX/SPX and NetBEUI.
- Disable unnecessary services that might provide unwanted access to server resources.
- Remove the POSIX and OS/2 subsystems, which might allow dangerous applications to be run on your server.
- Utilize the Windows 2000-assigned password for the Web guest account, `IUSR_computername`.
- Choose difficult passwords for all other accounts, including uppercase and lowercase letters, numerals, and special characters.
- Do not share directories for Microsoft networking using Server Message Block (SMB) access unless absolutely necessary. This includes removing the administrative shares, for example, C$, if you don't need them.
- If you do need to share directories through Microsoft networking, allow only authenticated users to connect to the shares. By default, Everyone is granted this access to the shares, but you should modify authorized users to only those who need access.
- Limit membership of the Administrator's group, and enforce strict account policies.
- Format all partitions as NTFS, and configure directory and file-level security.

Now that you have reviewed the general security recommendations for Windows 2000, this chapter will further discuss three specific topics: users and group accounts, NTFS security, and auditing and logging.

User and Group Accounts

All Windows 2000 resources, including those accessed using a Web browser, are represented as either data or an application object that can be accessed only by authorized Windows 2000 services and users. Anyone accessing Internet Information Services does so in the context of a user account—that is, the user accesses resources by submitting to it the security credentials of a user account configured in Windows 2000.

Access to each object is controlled through an access control list (ACL), which is a list of user accounts and their access rights to the object. Every user of the server will have a user account. When you grant directory and file-level permissions through NTFS, the user account is added to the file or directory's ACL along with the permissions you grant to that user account. When a user wants to access an object, the system checks the user's security identifier (SID) associated with the user account that the user is logged on with and associated group memberships, and then compares these identities with the object's ACL to determine whether the user is allowed to complete the request.

The association of an ACL with a file or directory is possible only with the NTFS file system. For this reason, it is the recommended file system for all Windows 2000–based systems, especially those that host Web sites. Implementing NTFS on a partition gives administrators precise control over files and directories on the partition.

It is common practice—and is strongly recommended by Microsoft—that you assign permissions to groups rather than users. Generally, permissions are not given to individual user accounts because of the complexity in managing permissions this way. However, under some circumstances you may need to establish permissions for users. It is perfectly legitimate to do so (and even I do this on occasion), but you must always be mindful of exactly what you did so that you don't later experience security problems that either deny—or, worse, allow—access when you didn't intend to.

User accounts can also be further secured by strict password rules, solid policies, and an understanding of access tokens. The remainder of this section discusses these topics.

Passwords

The Internet is accessed by millions of users, only a fraction of whom are hackers. Still, there are way too many for you to not be concerned about the vulnerability of your passwords. Again, each account used by Internet Information Services is a Windows 2000 account. Your concern shouldn't just be with the security of Internet Information Services, but should be with the security of your entire system.

First, you should utilize the password generated by the system for the `IUSR_computername` account. Because this password is created using an algorithm, it is as difficult to guess as you can get. Change it only if your environment requires you, as the administrator, to know the password. For example, it may need to duplicate the `IUSR_computername` account on another server in your environment and allow them to reference each other by having the same password. For all other accounts, though, use common sense and standard strong passwords, which should have the following characteristics:

- Five or more characters
- Mixed-case letters
- Alphanumeric characters
- Special characters

Logon Rights

Windows 2000 includes the capability to access a computer locally or remotely. Local users are also interactive users, typically those sitting at the console, but a local user can also be a service that runs from the local system. Remote users access the system from across the network using server message blocks (SMB).

When the Web service is started for a specific Web site, the service logs on to the Windows 2000 system by using the anonymous Web account. Because the Web service logs on to the local computer from the local computer, this access is considered local. Thus, the anonymous Web account must have permissions as an interactive user. Any account can be designated as an interactive account by modifying the Windows 2000 logon rights for that account or for a group to which that account belongs.

Because any user connecting to Internet Information Services is considered an interactive user, each account that is used to access a Web site must have logon rights to log on locally. Accounts that must have logon rights locally include those accessing a Web site through anonymous, basic or integrated Windows authentication. Also, as discussed in the next chapter, each account that is used to access an FTP site must have permissions as an interactive account.

Access Tokens

Each time an account logs on to a Windows 2000 system, it is given an *access token*, a set of properties that define its user ID, group memberships, and policies. This token is used for the entire session of an account logon and is presented to each object that the account needs to access. The properties of the access token are compared to the ACL of the object to determine whether the user should be granted access to the object.

When discussing Windows 2000 in a strict network environment, an access token is generated when a user account logs on to the system. When the logged on user attempts to access an object, this access token is compared to the ACL of the object. If the ACL for an object is changed while a user is logged on, then that the new security cannot be implemented because the user's access token is outdated. To flush the access token, the user must log off and log back on to the system (disconnect and reconnect).

When discussing Internet Information Services, the account used by the Web service to access the system is logged on when the Web service is started and is logged off when the service is stopped. The account used by the FTP service to access the

Additional Password Protection

You cannot view the passwords of Windows 2000 user accounts. Recall that in Windows NT, all accounts appeared with 14 asterisks in the password field. Either way, not only are all passwords hidden from system administrators, but they are also disguised so that not even the number of characters can be determined. When viewing passwords typed directly into the IIS snap-in (to the MMC), the password is still hidden and always contains 10 asterisks in the password field. This is a nice, and more secure, change from Internet Information Server 4, where the number of asterisks actually represented the number of characters in the password.

system is logged on when a user logs in to the FTP service and is logged off when a user logs off the FTP service. Thus, the most efficient way to flush the access token for an account accessing either of these services is to stop and start the Web or FTP service.

However, there are other occasions when the access token is flushed. By default, the access token used by the Web service is cached by the system for only 15 minutes. So, assume that you create a Web site that is rarely used. The anonymous Web account is configured as `IUSR_Website1`. When a user connects to the Web site from Internet Explorer, the account `IUSR_Website1` logs on to the Web service. The user continues to surf the site for 10 minutes, still using the cached access token. After the user leaves the site, no other user connects for half an hour. After 15 minutes of no activity, the access token will expire, and a new one will have to be generated for the next user. However, if the Web site is busy, the access token can be cached indefinitely.

Access tokens are important in Internet Information Services because they modify permissions, either within IIS or within Windows 2000. For example, suppose that the user in the previous scenario tries to access a Web page that `IUSR_Website1` does not have NTFS permissions to access. The user types the URL into Internet Explorer and receives the error message "Access Denied." You immediately modify the NTFS permissions to provide access to the file for the `IUSR_Website1` account. However, the user is still not able to access the Web page, because his access token has now become outdated. You should stop and start the Web service for the Web site to generate a new access token and, thus, reflect the account's new permissions. The more global service, IIS, runs as a local system account and is not affected by this issue.

If 15 minutes seems either too long or too short a timeout period for your Web site, you can change the default cache setting by modifying the `AccessTokenTTL` registry entry.

NTFS

NTFS, or NT File System, is the key to successfully protecting Internet Information Services and your Web sites while providing the access necessary for the user utilizing the Web server. NTFS was designed to provide security features for high-end servers and workstations, including those accessed from the Internet. When properly configured, Internet Information Services and Windows 2000 can be used to establish a safe environment for any documents publicly accessed.

For documents from IIS to be protected by Windows 2000 security, these files and directories need to be placed on an NTFS partition. By using NTFS, you ensure the access that users and groups need to the appropriate files and directories in Internet Information Services.

Similar Error Messages, Dissimilar Meanings

Although error messages, such as "Access Denied" and "Access Forbidden," may seem similar, they can identify very different issues. For example, when a Web browser returns the error "Access Denied," it is an indication that security settings do not allow access to the requested file. When a Web browser returns the error "Access Forbidden," it likely indicates that the requested file does not exist.

After IIS has validated a user's IP address and Internet domain, account and password, and Web or FTP permissions, it attempts to access the file based on the user's security context. Because the file is physically located on a hard drive within the server, and because Windows 2000 is the underlying operating system, IIS must make a request to Windows 2000 for the file. Windows 2000 then verifies that the user context has the correct NTFS permissions to access the file.

Recall that NTFS permissions include read (R), write (W), execute (X), delete (D) and change permissions (P), and take ownership (O). When these permissions are applied to files accessed by users of Internet Information Services, they provide users with different abilities, depending on the protocol used to access the file.

Some of the abilities provided to users accessing a Web site by using the HTTP protocol or accessing an FTP site by using the FTP protocol include those shown in Table 3.1. Note that different NTFS permissions allow different types of access for IIS users.

Table 3.1   **NTFS Permissions**

Permission	Description
Read (R)	Display physical directory listings
	View files, including text, graphics, and sounds
	Download files
Write (W)	Upload files
Execute (X)	Execute applications, including .exe and .dll files
	Execute scripts, including .asp files
Delete (D)	Delete a folder or a file
Change Permission	None
Take Ownership (O)	None

Validating a user's NTFS permissions is the last step that Internet Information Services takes when verifying that a user is allowed access to a resource. Therefore, you have the ability to configure other security options before NTFS permissions are ever consulted. However, because NTFS permissions are the final step, it can also be considered the final safety measure, sort of like a football team's kicker having the ultimate responsibility of making sure that the receiver does not return the ball for a touchdown.

After the permissions are established in IIS, the directories need to have their NTFS permissions configured in Windows 2000. Take these steps to accomplish this task:

1. From Windows Explorer, select the files or directory.

2. Right-click the file or directory, and click **Properties**.

3. Click the **Security** tab.

   If the Security tab does not appear on the Property sheet of a file or directory, the partition is not formatted with NTFS. In this case, reconsider making all partitions NTFS.

4. Configure the access permissions for the appropriate users and groups by selecting the user or group, and either clearing or selecting the appropriate permission's check box.

5. Check "Allow inheritable permissions from parent to propagate to this object" if you want this directory or file to get the same permissions as its parent.

6. For more granular access control, click the **Advanced** button.

7. In the Access Control Settings dialog box, select a user or group, and click **View/Edit** to configure specific permission. Click **OK** when you are finished with this dialog box.

8. When these steps are completed, close the Properties dialog box. Figure 3.2 shows a sample NTFS configuration.

It is important to remember that the security settings for Internet Information Services and Windows 2000 might conflict, particularly if someone configured the setup incorrectly. If these conflicts exist, the system will take the most restrictive settings.

It is also important to remember that, by default, the Everyone group has full control of all files and directories on newly created NTFS partitions. Refer to Chapter 1, "Installing and Managing IIS," for appropriately planning for Internet Information Services and configuring Windows 2000.

Auditing and Logging

After your security is configured, Windows 2000 provides several different methods to troubleshoot security issues and determine what happened. These methods can help you determine which accounts have logged on, or attempted to log on, to your server.

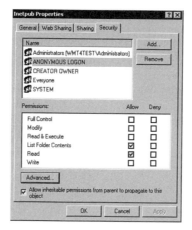

Figure 3.2   NTFS is used to secure files and directories for individual
user access to Internet Information Services.

It can also determine which pages and files have been accessed, as well as any patterns in accesses or access attempts.

Methods for auditing and logging access to Internet Information Services include Windows 2000 Event Logging and Internet Information Services Logging. Internet Information Services Logging is covered in a later chapter.

All auditing and logging should be configured for either the IUSR_computername account or for the special group Everyone. Generally, if you are auditing or troubleshooting a Web-related issue, auditing the IUSR_computername account will tell you what the anonymous Web user is doing. Auditing this account compared to auditing the Everyone special group also reduces the system resources required for auditing. If you need more information than that one account can provide, then auditing the Everyone special group will tell you about all accounts accessing the IIS computer.

If you plan a detailed security policy, you can also audit for a defined group of users. For example, you can create a group called Internet Access and populate it with the anonymous account and all other accounts to which you have provided nonanonymous access. Then, you can audit this group, which provides more information than just auditing the anonymous account, but requires fewer resources than auditing the Everyone special group.

When configuring Windows 2000 auditing and logging on a Web server, some options include these:

- **Audit account logon events.** It is a best practice to audit all failed account logon and logoff attempts to a Web server. Successful logon and logoff attempts can tell you which accounts are accessing your server and when the Web and FTP services log on. However, failed logon attempts can tell you who is attempting to compromise the security of your Web server, or who is attempting to access objects that they do not have permission to access.

  In the case of the latter, a user attempting to access a secure Web page may use integrated Windows authentication and unknowingly pass his local account information to your Web server. An unsuccessful logon attempt will appear in the Windows 2000 Event log with the user's local account name.

- **Audit directory service access.** Auditing file and object access allows you to determine who is accessing—or, more importantly, attempting to access—a specific file or folder. This type of auditing is best used to track down attempted security breaches.

  If practical, audit only failed access attempts to files and folders. Successful access to objects could consume your entire Event Log in hours, if not minutes, depending on your Web server traffic and the files and folders that you choose to audit. And be honest—you probably won't ever look at all those "good" messages.

Figure 3.3 displays the Audit Policy dialog box in Windows 2000.

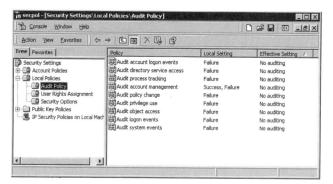

Figure 3.3 Use Windows 2000 Event logs to audit security on Internet Information Services.

Security Planning

Carefully plan the setup of IIS to best protect the perused site. For example, keep executable files and text/graphics files in separate directories so that you can easily provide different levels of access. Also, anonymous users generally need only read permission, as established in both Internet Information Services and in Windows 2000.

Security settings for the IIS directories should be established based on the type of directory. If the directory is content-based, the observer should have read (R) access. If the directory is program-based, the observer should have read and execute (RX) access. If the directory is a database, the observer should have read and write (RW) access. That is, the following permissions are recommended:

Content	Read access (R)
Programs	Read and execute access (RX)
Databases	Read and write access (RW)

This is recommended for the user accounts that will be accessing the data. Web site administrators that will be modifying this data require write and delete permissions to the directories.

Now that you have reviewed Windows 2000 security, you are ready to tackle the next topic, Internet Information Services security.

Additional Resources

For further reading and information about Internet Information Services security, check out the *Internet Information Services 5.0 Resource Guide* in the Windows 2000 Resource Kit from Microsoft Press. You can also access the Microsoft Security Web Site at http://www.microsoft.com/security/. If you plan to administer an IIS server (or any Microsoft server, for that matter), you should frequently refer to this Web site.

4

IIS Security

AS AN APPLICATION, INTERNET INFORMATION SERVICES provides its own security methods. And because these security features work together with those provided in the base operating system, a good understanding of Windows 2000 security is necessary before you can configure Internet Information Services security. If you skipped over the last chapter and don't have a strong understanding of Windows 2000 security, go back and review it before proceeding.

This chapter covers the following topics:

- How Internet Information Services security functions, and how it relates to Windows 2000 security
- The role of IP address and domain name restrictions
- Internet Information Services access permissions and their relationship to NTFS permissions
- The methods of user authentication in Internet Information Services 5
- Impersonation and its effect on remote access privileges

Internet Information Services Security with Windows 2000

Recall from Chapter 3, "Integrating IIS with Windows 2000 Security," that Internet Information Services utilizes a four-step process in controlling Web site access. That chapter discussed the two steps based on Windows 2000 security features.

This chapter focuses on the other two steps, which are provided by Internet Information Services:

1. Checks for specific IP restrictions
2. Verifies Web site permissions

Figure 4.1 shows a graphical representation of the Internet Information Services security process.[1]

In addition to discussing this process, this chapter devotes considerable time to discussing access control. *Access control* is the method by which Internet Information Services identifies the user connecting to the Web or FTP service. After the user is identified and verified, IIS can leverage Windows 2000 security features for both the account permissions and NTFS permissions. These Windows 2000 security features

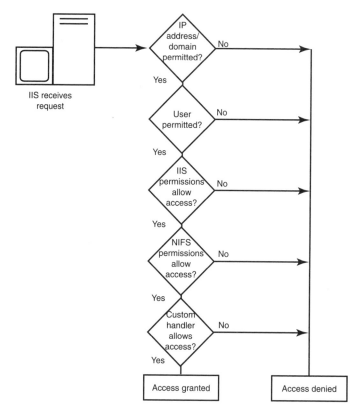

Figure 4.1 The first two steps in the IIS security process are performed by Internet Information Services.

---

[1] Note that in Figure 4.1, there are five steps instead of four. In addition to the standard steps, IIS gives you the flexibility of creating your own custom security handler.

were discussed in the previous chapter. This chapter focuses on the methodology of identifying the account and the characteristics of each account.

IP Address and Domain Name Restrictions

The first step in the Internet Information Services security process is to validate that the source IP address and/or source domain name are permitted to access the requested Web site. Using IP address and domain name restrictions, you can grant or deny specific computers, groups of computers, or domains access to your Web site.

By default, Internet Information Services allows all IP addresses and source domains to access all Web sites, except the Administration Web Site created by Internet Information Services. You can then configure which IP addresses and source domains to deny access to. You could, instead, reverse this process and deny access to all IP addresses and source domains initially, and specify those that are allowed access. See Figure 4.2 as a refresher of your configuration options.

After determining whether all computers are granted or denied access, you can configure the following exceptions:

- Single computer
- Group of computers
- Domain name

To grant or deny access to a single computer, click the **Single Computer** radio button. The subsequent dialog box provides two options for specifying the computer: the IP Address text box or the DNS Lookup button.

To specify the computer by IP address, simply type the address into the text box. To specify the computer by fully qualified domain name (FQDN), such as hacker.kadam.com, click the **DNS Lookup** button, and type the name into the Enter the DNS Name text box. Internet Information Services immediately executes an NSLOOKUP to resolve the FQDN to an IP address, and then automatically inputs the resolved IP address into the IP Address text box.

Figure 4.2   Internet Information Services can be configured to restrict
access based on a client's source IP address or domain.

Because of this resolution method, if the IP address for the specified computer is later changed, the restriction will no longer be active, just like specifying an IP address to begin with. Unfortunately, changing a source IP address is about as easy as changing your screen colors, so the true level of security here is minimal.

To grant or deny access to a group of computers, click the **Group of Computers** radio button. You can then type the group's network ID and associated subnet mask in their respective text boxes. See Figure 4.3 for an example of a valid configuration.

The network ID means just that—the ID of the entire network, or subnet, that will be granted or denied access. A valid network ID is determined by the subnet mask associated with it. For example, if you want to deny access to all computers with the IP addresses of 192.168.10.1 through 192.168.10.254, you need to input the network ID of 192.168.10.0 and a subnet mask of 255.255.255.0. This combination of subnet mask and network ID results in host IDs ranging from 1 to 254 in the fourth octet. The same rules apply to a network with a custom subnet mask. For example, only computers with host IP addresses of 209.67.73.65 though 209.67.73.94 will be denied access to the Web site if you configure a combination of network ID 209.67.73.64 with a subnet mask of 255.255.255.224. This combination results in host IDs of 65 through 94 in the fourth octet. For further explanation of subnetting, see the concise discussion of it in the *Microsoft TCP/IP Training* self-study kit from Microsoft Press.

Be careful, though. If you input a host IP address instead of a network ID, based on the subnet mask, then Internet Information Services will grant or deny access only to that specific host. So, if in the previous example you had input a network ID of 192.138.10.1 and a subnet mask of 255.255.255.0, you would be denying access only to a host with an IP address of 192.138.10.1, not all hosts on its subnet.

To grant or deny access to all computers within a single domain, click the **Domain Name** radio button. In the new text box, type the source domain name for any host that you want to grant or deny access to. For example, you could type a full domain, such as `microsoft.com` or a subdomain, such as `training.microsoft.com`. Internet Information Services then executes a DNS reverse resolution to determine the FQDN of the requesting host. Again, this process brings up a few issues.

If you grant or deny access to computers specified by a domain name, Internet Information Services will need to determine the source domain name of each client

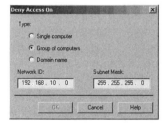

Figure 4.3   Configure access for a group of computers
by defining the group's subnet ID.

that attempts to access your site, and this is not a simple process. Immediately after selecting the **Domain Name** radio button, you will see Internet Information Services pop up a message that reads:

> Warning: Restricting access by domain name requires a DNS reverse lookup on each connection. This is a very expensive operation and will dramatically affect server performance.

Also, the requesting host must be configured with a domain name. Although many clients connecting from within large corporations can be resolved to a domain name, many other clients on the Internet cannot, and thus cannot be evaluated based on domain name. If you choose to restrict access by domain name and the client cannot be resolved to a domain name, Internet Information Services will fail to validate the domain and will fail to deny access to the client.

Again, validation of the client's IP address and domain name is only the first step in a series of steps you can take to permit or deny access to a Web page. It is certainly not the most secure of these steps. Hackers on the Internet can easily change or spoof their source IP address or domain name and render this entire step worthless. So, granting access to all IP addresses and domain names and only restricting a few is relatively ineffective.

A more effective use of IP address and domain name restrictions is to initially deny access to all source IP addresses and domain names, and then permit access to only those few that require access. This scenario is still vulnerable to IP address and domain name spoofing, but a hacker would need to determine one of those few valid IP addresses or domain names allowed access to the Web site. In the scope of the entire Internet, a hacker would need to find a needle in a haystack. Also, because IP address and domain name spoofing is much rarer in an intranet environment than on the Internet, restricting access by IP address and domain name provides the most value in an intranet environment. For example, if you need to place a secured Web site on an intranet when the Web site should be accessible only by one department, you may have the ability to restrict access to the department's subnet or to the department's subdomain, depending on the configuration of the company's network.

For example, suppose that you work at a large corporation and create a Web site that should be accessible only to others in your department. If all computers in the department are in the domain `training.connectos.com` or are on the same subnet, you can configure Internet Information Services to deny access to all computers except those in your local domain or on your local subnet.

Access Permissions

Access permissions in Internet Information Services refer to the capability of the Web client to use the file and directory resources within a Web site. These permissions include the capability to read a file, to write a file, to receive script source access, or to allow directory browsing. Internet Information Services 5 enables you to specify the access permissions for each virtual server or Web site and each virtual directory that you create. Figure 4.4 displays the Web site property sheet that you will use to specify access permissions for a virtual server.

Internet Information Services access permissions are independent of NTFS file permissions, although there is a relationship within Internet Information Services. As you saw in Figure 4.1, the third step in the Internet Information Services security process is to verify the access permissions configured within IIS.

The fourth step in this process is to verify the NTFS permissions for the same resource. For example, when a Web client attempts to access the file `default.asp` in a Web site, Internet Information Services first verifies that the Web client has read access permissions to the directory as configured in the Web site Properties page. After validating this permission, Internet Information Services then requests the file from the Windows 2000 operating system. Assuming, and hoping, that the file is located in a NTFS partition, Windows 2000 then verifies that the Web client has read permissions within the file system. If either of these permissions do not allow the Web client to read the file, then permission is denied to the Web client. So, by definition, the *effective permissions* are the most restrictive of Internet Information Services access permissions and NTFS permissions.

In addition to the standard read access permissions, Internet Information Services enables you to control three other types of access: write permission, directory browsing, and script source access.

- **Write permission.** Allows a Web client to submit new files to the directory or change an existing file. Beginning with Internet Information Server 4, HTTP PUT allows HTTP 1.1-compliant Web clients, such as Internet Explorer 5, to post information to a Web site using the standard HTTP protocol.

Figure 4.4   Access permissions for a virtual server are configured on the Home Directory tab of the Default Web Site Properties sheet.

- **Directory browsing.** Allows a Web client to receive the directory file listing if the specific file that it requested is not available. For example, when searching for information on a Web site, it is common for a Web user to erase the end of a URL to move up the Web site tree and navigate the site. If the user attempts to access a directory that does not contain a default Web page, such as `default.asp` or `default.htm`, the Web browser will receive a listing of all files within that directory if directory browsing is enabled.

  Generally speaking, directory browsing is considered a security risk and should not be enabled unless you intend to provide any Web user with a list of all files in your Web site.

- **Script source access.** Allows a Web client to read or change source code for scripts, such as those in an ASP application, if either read or write permission is also enabled. It is a new access permission in Internet Information Services 5. Again, enabling this check box would most likely create a security risk, and it should not be enabled unless you have evaluated the consequences.

An additional access permission on the Home Directory tab in Internet Information Services 5 is execute permissions for applications. These permissions are unique in that they apply to applications instead of files and directories. In Internet Information Services 5, you can select None, Scripts only, or Scripts and Executables. In Internet Information Server 4, these same permissions were called eXecute and Script, and you could select one or the other, both, or neither. Because these permissions are different, they are covered in Chapter 7, "Running Web Applications."

Authentication

The synergy between Internet Information Services and Windows 2000 provides for some of the most powerful access control functionality of any Web server on the Internet. You can control access to files, folders, and applications by using a variety of security mechanisms. But the most important of these is the capability to control access for individual users and groups of users. The previous chapter discussed NTFS security as the heart of Internet Information Services security. To take advantage of this feature, Internet Information Services must first identify the user connecting to the service.

In Internet Information Services 5, you can select among four different access control methods. The first three were also included in previous versions of Internet Information Services. They are anonymous access, integrated Windows authentication (previously called Windows NT Challenge/Response), and basic authentication. The fourth method, digest authentication for Windows domain servers, is new in Internet Information Services 5. Also of note because of its increasing popularity is Fortezza authentication, or smart cards, which will be discussed last. Figure 4.5 displays these options as they can be selected with the new interface. The following sections discuss how each of these methods work and cover the nuances of each.

Figure 4.5   The Authentication Methods dialog box lets you select one or more of the four methods available in Internet Information Services 5.

All users accessing Internet Information Services are either anonymous users or nonanonymous users. When a user attempts to connect to a Web site, Internet Information Services attempts to validate the user in the following order:

1. Anonymous access

2. Integrated Windows authentication

3. Basic authentication

Anonymous Access

When asking my students which account is used to log users on to Windows 2000 when accessing the WWW service, most guess the GUEST account. Some even guess none, which is a perfect time for me to launch into a discussion of basic Windows 2000 security—but I won't now. The answer, of course, depends on how Internet Information Services has been configured. For now, however, simply assume that it is freshly loaded and using the defaults.

The anonymous account is often called the IUSR account (pronounced "I-user"), after the default anonymous account of `IUSR_computername`. However, any account can be the anonymous account. As long as the account exists in the security account manager (SAM) database within Windows 2000 and possesses permissions to log on interactively, it can be configured as the anonymous user account in Internet Information Services. I've even seen someone use the Administrator account, although they had no idea what they had done.

For the WWW service, all Web client logon requests are initiated as an anonymous logon. For the FTP service, you are prompted for an account name and password when you connect to the server. You have the option of logging on anonymously by entering a username of either anonymous or ftp, and any password you choose. With either service, when you've indicated that you want to log on anonymously, the password is irrelevant. No password is sent with the WWW service, and the password you send with the FTP service is logged, but not validated. You couldn't possibly know the anonymous password for every WWW and FTP server on the Internet, and because the server is letting you log on without validating who you are, there is no need to request a password from you. However, it is good netiquette to enter your email name as your password for FTP connections. It gives the Web master some idea of who you are.

In Internet Information Services 5, the check box for "Allow Internet Information Services to control password" in the Anonymous User Account dialog box is enabled by default. The most obvious question is, what does Internet Information Services do with the account? The surprising answer is "nothing." If you change the password for the anonymous user account in Windows 2000 Computer Management program, there is no need to stop or start any Internet Information Services, because the password is not actually changed in Internet Information Services. The password was never there to begin with, so it doesn't get updated.

But the big question regarding anonymous access has always been, at least in my mind, what is the password for the `IUSR_computername` account? Or, at least, how can I figure it out? Unfortunately, I now have it on good authority from a security guru at Microsoft that the password is, and I quote, "random goo." In layman's terms, the password for the `IUSR_computername` is a random combination of letters, numerals, and punctuation marks generated when Internet Information Services is installed. This does mean that it can, on occasion, become all letters, all numerals, or even all punctuation marks, but that's not only very rare, but also very irrelevant. It's basically unhackable.

Integrated Windows Authentication

Integrated Windows authentication, previously called Windows NT Challenge/Response (NTLM), is the most secure method of authentication not only because it requires a valid user account in Windows 2000, but also because the password is never transmitted across the network. With Integrated Windows authentication, the client uses its current username and password to attempt authentication with Internet Information Services. After it's authenticated, the requested resource is accessed in the context of the specified user.

To utilize integrated Windows authentication, many pieces must be configured and must work together. The following steps outline the process used to authenticate a user with integrated Windows authentication:

1. A client requests a connection to the Web site from Internet Information Services.

2. Internet Information Services attempts to authenticate the anonymous user account, assuming that one is configured in IIS, because anonymous access is always the first authentication method.

3. When anonymous access is denied, or if anonymous access is not configured for the Web site, Internet Information Services informs the client that it can

validate access via integrated Windows authentication, if the client supports this authentication method.

4. Internet Information Services then issues a challenge number to the Web client in an attempt to validate the client's current username and password using integrated Windows authentication. If those credentials are rejected, Internet Information Services will prompt the user for a name and password by means of a dialog box.

5. The Web client then hashes this number with the local user account's password. The user account and result of this hash are then sent back to Internet Information Services.

6. Internet Information Services in turn takes the same number that it sent to the client and hashes it with the password of the user account from the SAM database. IIS then compares the results of its hash with the results of the client hash. If the hashes match, Windows 2000 determines that the passwords must be the same, and Windows 2000 authenticates the user.

The key to integrated Windows authentication is that the user's password is never actually sent to the Web server. This negates any concern about encryption of the password or packet sniffing being used to discover the password. You might think that because the password is not actually submitted to Internet Information Services, and thus Windows 2000, there is the possibility that the hash would match but the passwords would not. And you're right. However, the chances of this occurring are about 1 in 2^{128}. An equally important issue though, is that because Internet Information Services does not have knowledge of the user's password, it cannot pass these credentials on to any other server, including a server that houses a remote virtual directory.

Supporting Integrated Windows authentication as a client requires two technologies. First, the client must be using an advanced Microsoft operating system. Integrated Windows authentication is supported in Windows 2000, Windows NT, and Windows 95 and later with the Client for Microsoft Networks installed. Secondly, the client must be using a Web browser that supports integrated Windows authentication. At this time, only Microsoft Internet Explorer version 2.0 and later support this authentication method. Also, keep in mind that because of the two-way communication process required to successfully complete integrated Windows authentication, this authentication method is not supported through a firewall or a proxy server.

Basic Authentication

The third method is basic authentication. With basic authentication, the user is prompted for a username and password when accessing a resource. This makes some

Challenge Numbers in Internet Information Services 5

A *challenge number* is a long, random number generated by an algorithm. The challenge number generated by Internet Information Services 5 changes with each authentication request.

users feel more secure because their browser actually pops up a dialog box in which they can manually input information. However, this is the most insecure of the four methods.

With basic authentication, the username and password are transmitted to the server in clear text or Base64-encoded. When transmitting in clear text, the password is unencrypted and, thus, can be easily intercepted by potential hackers. Because the user account must be a valid account in the Windows 2000 SAM, a successful hacker would not only have access to Internet Information Services, but also potentially to your entire server.

When Internet Information Services receives the username and password, it verifies these credentials against the local Windows 2000 SAM database, the local Windows 2000 domain SAM database, or the SAM database of any trusted Windows domains. If the credentials are validated, IIS impersonates the user when accessing files and resources. So, whether the user is accessing an ISAPI application, script, or file, IIS presents the user's credentials to the resource, including to NTFS in the case of a file. It is important to note that with basic authentication, Internet Information Services actually receives the password for the user account. Later, this chapter discusses how IIS has a lot more flexibility with accounts when it has knowledge of the user's password.

To utilize basic authentication in Internet Information Services, three things must be configured. First, the username and password entered into the dialog box must exist as a valid Windows 2000 account in the SAM database. Secondly, this account must have interactive rights. Finally, basic authentication must be enabled in Internet Information Services for the Web site. Refer back to Figure 4.5 to review the screen for enabling basic authentication.

Digest Authentication

Like integrated Windows authentication, digest authentication uses hashing technology to secure password and user account information from being transmitted over the network. Unlike integrated Windows authentication, however, digest authentication is capable of traversing proxy server and firewall boundaries with ease. To use digest authentication, you must be part of a Windows 2000 domain, and the user must be using Internet Explorer 5.0 or later. For more information about the digest authentication extension to the HTTP standard, see the Digest Authentication Proposal at http://www.ics.uci.edu/pub/ietf/http/rfc2069.txt.

Authenticating Netscape Navigator Clients

Of the four authentication methods available in Internet Information Services 5, only two are supported by Netscape Navigator clients. Anonymous authentication is supported by all Web clients, because the authentication is completely handled by the Web server. Netscape clients can also be authenticated by using basic authentication because basic simply transmits a username and password that were entered into a dialog box. So, if you must validate a nonanonymous user from a Netscape client, basic authentication is the only solution, but the security implications are strong and should be heavily weighed.

Fortezza Authentication

Fortezza authentication is the last authentication method discussed. However, after reviewing the Directory Security tab in Figure 4.5, you will notice that is not included as one of the four authentication methods in Internet Information Services 5. Still, because of its unique capability to authenticate users and because it is supported by Internet Information Services 5, it is mentioned here.

Fortezza is a U.S. government security standard that, among other things, enables you to use the new smart card technology to determine the identity of users. Smart cards contain either a magnetic strip or a computer chip with a client certificate that can be used to validate the identity of the user making requests. The user swipes the card through a reader attached to the server or network, and the authentication takes place. This certificate functions in a similar way to standard server or client certificates. For more information on how certificates function in Internet Information Services 5, see Chapter 9, "SSL and Certificate Services."

Use of Fortezza with Internet Information Services 5 requires a non-export copy of `Schannel.dll` from Microsoft's Web site, a card reader and its drivers, and a cryptographic service provider (CSP) to use with the card reader. After the card reader is installed and configured, you will use the `Fortutil.exe` that ships with Internet Information Services 5 to install, confirm, or delete the card certificate. For more information about Fortezza, see the Fortezza Web site at `http://www.armadillo.huntsville.al.us/`. For more information about using Fortezza with Internet Information Services 5, see the online documentation.

Selecting an Authentication Method

To determine the method to use for your site, find the scenario in those that follow that most closely matches your site, and configure your authentication accordingly. For more information on configuring these methods, see the Internet Information Services 5 documentation:

- **Public Internet site with only public information.** There's no need to know who is requesting resources; use anonymous authentication.

- **Public Internet site with some private information.** Put public content in one directory and the private information in another, and assign NTFS permissions as stated earlier. Use anonymous authentication for public areas and another secure authentication method for private information.

- **Private Internet site (extranet or WAN).** If there is no firewall and users have Internet Explorer 2.0 or later, use integrated Windows authentication. If all users are using Internet Explorer 5.0, the server is a member of a Windows 2000 domain, and you have a firewall, use digest authentication.

- **Public intranet site.** If there is no firewall and users have Internet Explorer 2.0 or later, use integrated Windows authentication. Anonymous authentication will also work, but integrated is just as easy and more secure. If there is a firewall between the server and users, then you can use anonymous authentication.

- **Ultra-secure sites (if you're the CIA or something).** For absolutely secure authentication, use one-to-one client certificate mapping or Fortezza authentication. These methods are great, because user information is absolutely secure, unless you give your certificate or card to someone.

Impersonation

As discussed in the "Authentication" section, a client is logged on to the Web or FTP service with either an anonymous or a nonanonymous user account. After the client logs on, Internet Information Services accesses all files and applications in the security context of that local user account—that is, the user it considers physically logged on the server. This functionality is called *impersonation* and allows the administrator to control access based on this account. However, in addition to being used with local resources, these credentials can be delegated to another server when it is accessed by the same user session. The rest of this chapter explores the concept of delegating credentials from Internet Information Services.

When Internet Information Services is first installed, it registers a subauthentication DLL (dynamic link library) with the Windows 2000 operating system. Then, whenever a Web or FTP client connects to Internet Information Services, Windows 2000 calls into the DLL to verify the user account submitted by the client.

The subauthentication DLL performs a network logon, not a local logon. Unfortunately, however, a network logon cannot delegate credentials. This means that any user authenticated in this manner cannot pass credentials to another server, including one housing a remote virtual directory. The functionality of the subauthentication DLL is loosely similar to the functionality of transient trusts in Windows NT domains—it just doesn't work that way.

If Internet Information Services is explicitly submitted an account and password as part of a local logon, these credentials can be submitted to another computer one hop away, meaning connected to the same local network. All basic logons are local logons. However, anonymous logons without "Allow IIS to control password" enabled are local logons, but anonymous logons with the "Allow IIS to control password" check box selected are generated as network logons by using the subauthentication DLL discussed previously. When the "Allow IIS to control password" check box is selected, IIS

Adding Secure Sockets Layer

Secure Sockets Layer (SSL) is an additional level of security that encrypts data transferred across the network, as well as user account and password information. It is a desirable option for all private Web sites, both on the Internet and on an intranet. For information on SSL, see Chapter 9.

never receives or verifies the password, so these credentials cannot be delegated. Also, because integrated Windows authentication never submits a password with the account name, its credentials cannot be delegated. See Table 4.1 for a summary of the different authentication methods and their capability to delegate credentials to servers running related services, such as databases. Note that not all authentication methods can delegate the user account and password to nearby servers.

The Anonymous account can be configured to pass its credentials to another computer one hop away by simply disabling "Allow IIS to control password." The client is then logged on locally with the anonymous account because the password configured in Internet Information Services is submitted with the account to Windows 2000. The end result is the same as that of accessing the Web site anonymously with "Allow IIS to control password" enabled, except that the credentials can now be passed to another computer. But one minor issue stops most administrators from disabling "Allow IIS to control password"—that is the administrative headache of manually synchronizing the IUSR password in Internet Information Services and Windows 2000, and then troubleshooting the problems resulting from an unsynchronized password.

For example, let's say that Michael connects to a Web site as the anonymous user. In this case, the anonymous user is configured with IIS controlling the password. Michael's attempted logon uses the `IUSR_computername` account. IIS first calls into Windows 2000 with the account name to verify that the user account exists in the SAM database. Windows 2000 in turn captures the logon user call and calls into the subauthentication DLL for verification. Because it is in a trusted piece of code, Windows 2000 authenticates the user and generates an access token, all without ever verifying the password.

Now suppose that Michael clicks on a link to a Microsoft SQL Server database that requires authentication based on the current user context. Because the anonymous user account is not considered to be logged on locally, and because Windows 2000 never actually validated the password, the current credentials cannot be passed on to the remote SQL Server. But had IIS not been allowed to control the password, Windows 2000 would have received and validated the password, and the anonymous user credentials could then have been submitted to the remote SQL Server.

Table 4.1 **Authentication Methods**

Authentication Method	Delegate Credentials?
Anonymous *with* "Allow IIS to control password"	No
Anonymous *without* "Allow IIS to control password"	Yes—one hop
Integrated Windows authentication	No
Basic authentication	Yes—one hop

So far, you've learned about planning and installing Internet Information Services in Chapter 1, "Installing and Managing IIS;" positioning it on the Internet in Chapter 2, "Internetworking Considerations;" and using security options in Chapter 3, "Integrating IIS with Windows 2000 Security," and Chapter 4, "IIS Security." Now you're ready to learn how to configure Web and FTP sites.

5

Customizing WWW Sites

NOW THAT YOU'VE SPENT A CONSIDERABLE amount of time preparing Internet Information Services, you're ready to start configuring it. For most administrators, this means adding and configuring Web sites. This chapter covers specific issues related to customizing Web sites in Internet Information Services. It does *not* outline the basics of setting up a Web site, and it does not discuss every single dialog box and text box available in the IIS snap-in of Microsoft Management Console.

This chapter, like later chapters, assumes that you are already familiar with the basics of Internet Information Services. So, if you haven't yet set up a Web site, first review that information. A good beginner's choice is the Microsoft Internet Information Services Training Kit from Microsoft Press.

This chapter covers the following topics:

- The function of HTTP clients and servers
- How physical servers, virtual servers, physical directories, and virtual directories interact
- How to delegate limited administrative privileges to individual Web sites
- Issues and concerns when working with local and remote directories of any type
- How to exploit the new capabilities of HTTP 1.1, and how it functions between servers and clients
- The new configuration option for application server extensions

Under the Hood of HTTP

HTTP is a generic, stateless, object-oriented protocol. It is a client/server protocol located in the Application layer of the Internet protocol stack and communicates with WinSock. WinSock, or the Windows Sockets API, is a transport-level application programming interface created by Microsoft to allow third-party vendors to create applications that can easily communicate with the Windows operating system. WinSock is an extension to Berkeley Sockets, a core API developed in the UNIX environment. Moving down the protocol stack, WinSock communicates with the communication protocols on the Windows operating system, including TCP/IP. Figure 5.1 diagrams this communication.

The remainder of this section provides a detailed discussion of how different technologies play a role in Web communication. First, it looks at the components of a URL, and then covers the steps required to access a Web server.

Web clients attempt to access a Web server by typing a URL into a Web browser. For example, the complete URL to the ConnectOS Corporation home page is `http://www.connectos.com/default.htm`.

However, you could type the following into most browsers and receive the same results: `connectos.com`.

What happened to the other pieces of information? It takes several technologies to slim down this amount of typing. The following list briefly describes the role of each technology in this process.

- Most Web browsers, including Internet Explorer, assume that HTTP is the protocol if none is specified.

- A DNS server can be configured to reference a specific IP address if no host name, such as www, is specified.

- Internet Information Services can be configured to return a specific Web page, such as `default.htm`, if none is specified.

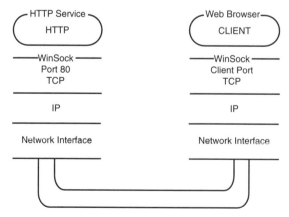

Figure 5.1   A Web client accesses a Web server by using HTTP, TCP, and IP.

Most users don't like to type long addresses, so knowing how to take advantage of the different technologies can ease this burden for everyone.

After a client types a URL into a Web browser, Internet Explorer formulates the data into a request. For example, a user types `http://www.msn.com/default.asp` into the Web browser. Several steps occur, and many more packets are sent before the client sees the returned Web page. The following list summarizes the typical steps a Web client takes to access an Internet Web site:

1. Internet Explorer formulates an HTTP/Request and passes it to the WinSock API.

2. WinSock determines that the destination is a fully qualified domain name (FQDN). DNS then requests and receives the IP address mapped to the FQDN.

3. WinSock passes the request to TCP using the newly discovered IP address of the destination server.

4. TCP assigns the connection a client port number and passes the request to IP.

5. IP evaluates the destination subnet against the source subnet and refers to the routing table, if necessary.

6. IP requests that the Address Resolution Protocol (ARP) determine the network adapter address of either the destination server, if it is on the local subnet, or the next router, if the destination server is on a remote subnet.

7. The data is formulated into a data packet and is passed to the Network Interface layer.

This process jumps into the depths of TCP/IP and protocol communication. If you read through it and thought, "What is a client port number?", "Isn't it TCP/IP—why do you mention TCP and IP separately?", or "What routing table?", then you should read up on TCP/IP. Understanding the lower levels of HTTP communication are fundamental to your ability to manage and troubleshoot Internet Information Services.

Organization of Sites

All Web sites may be formed from four different organizational structures: physical servers, virtual servers, physical directories, or virtual directories. An individual Web site is usually created as either a physical server or a virtual server, and either may additionally use a combination of physical and virtual directories. Figure 5.2 displays how three of the structures appear in the IIS snap-in for the MMC.

> **W3C**
>
> The World Wide Web Consortium (W3C) was founded in 1994 to develop common standards for the Web, including HTML and HTTP. You can find more information about the W3C on the W3C Web site at `http://www.w3.org/` or on the WWW mailing list from the W3C at `www-talk@w3.org`.

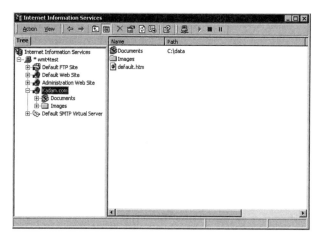

Figure 5.2 Virtual servers, physical directories, and virtual directories are monitored and managed through the IIS snap-in for MMC.

Physical Servers

The simplest organization of a single Web site is to host it alone on a computer. In this case, the Web site is associated with a physical computer and, thus, is a physical server. Most users on the Internet assume that all Web sites are physical servers because they contain a unique URL and IP address—and, of course, because many users are not familiar with the concept of virtual servers. However, the costs involved in running a single Web site as a physical server can be prohibitive to most businesses and individuals, which leads many to use a virtual server instead.

Virtual Servers

Internet Information Services allows you to have multiple IP addresses on a single physical computer. When a separate DNS record references each, it will appear that there are multiple Web servers. These kinds of Web sites are known as *virtual servers*, or Web server instances.

For example, suppose that you configure two IP addresses on a new computer. You can then use the IIS snap-in of Microsoft Management Console to create two Web sites. You configure the first Web site to use the first IP address and the second Web site to use the second IP address. Now your computer services HTTP requests for two separate Web sites. When you add the appropriate DNS entries to point www.connectos.com to the first IP address and www.kirkland.net to the second IP address, clients can access http://www.connectos.com/ and http://www.kirkland.net/ on the same computer. To the client, however, each site still appears to stand alone.

Assigning an IP Address

Each virtual server requires its own IP address. When you create a new Web site, you must specify which IP address is associated with that Web site.

Each IP address that you assign to a Web site must first be configured in Windows 2000. To assign multiple IP addresses to one computer running Windows 2000, perform the following steps:

1. Open Network and Dial-up Connections.
2. Right-click the local area connection, and then click **Properties**.
3. On the **General** tab, click **Internet Protocol (TCP/IP)**, and then click **Properties**.
4. Click **Advanced** to configure additional IP addresses and their corresponding subnet addresses.

Although this procedure is a bit different in Windows NT, the discussion of virtual servers in previous versions of Internet Information Services and IP addresses in Windows NT is the same.

After configuring multiple IP addresses for a Windows 2000 computer, you must then specify which IP address should be used for each Web site. Generally, you can use the IP Address drop-down list box on the Web Site tab of the Web site Properties page to select the IP address of the Web site. However, not all IP addresses may be in the list. If the IP address you need to assign is not listed, you need to manually type it in.

For one virtual server, you should specify "All unassigned" in the IP address box instead of assigning a specific IP address. This site, in essence, is designated as a default Web site that is accessed if a user attempts to connect to an IP address that is configured in Windows 2000 but not assigned to a Web site. This is necessary because common sense tells you to configure more IP addresses in Windows 2000 than you need in the foreseeable future. When you have assigned all the configured IP addresses to virtual servers, you will need to add more to Windows 2000. Of course, you should always reboot of the server after you add the new IP addresses, even if the operating system doesn't require it. So, if you don't want to reboot your Web server and take down all your virtual servers each time you need to add a new IP address, give yourself some room to grow.

When Internet Information Services receives a request for a Web page, the request specifies the IP address of the target Web server. It then locates the virtual server associated with that IP address and returns the requested Web page. Figure 5.3 displays the dialog box for this configuration. Although IP addresses appear in the drop-down

Number of IP Addresses

Microsoft Windows 2000 supports a virtually unlimited number of IP addresses on a single network adapter. It is certainly possible to add an entire Class C of IP addresses (about 254) to one network card, and thus support that many virtual servers on one computer.

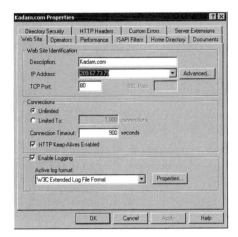

Figure 5.3 Specify a unique IP address for each Web site by using the IIS snap-in for the MMC.

box, know that not all IP addresses configured in the operating system will appear, so you may have to do a little typing.

Assigning a Domain Name

After the IP address is configured in Windows 2000 and you have assigned the IP address to a specific Web site, you need to make each Web site available to Web users by assigning it a domain name. For example, suppose that you configure both 10.10.10.100 and 10.20.20.100 in Windows 2000. You then create two Web sites in Internet Information Services and assign each of them one of the configured IP addresses. Finally, you configure two different domain name server (DNS) zones, one for each site, and create a resource record in each that points to the IP address assigned in Internet Information Services. Thus, it appears to users on the Internet that there are two computers—each running a single Web site—when in fact there is only one computer running one copy of the WWW service.

Physical Directories

All Web sites, whether created on a physical server or as a virtual server, will use at least one physical directory. This physical directory exists on the hard drive of a server, whether it is the one running Internet Information Services or is a remote one and is assigned as the home directory of the Web site. If you would like to review information on this structure, refer back to Chapter 2, "Internetworking Considerations."

All physical directories within a Web site are accessible from within that Web site. For example, suppose that a Web site home directory points to the D:\InetPub\kirkland.net directory. Within this physical directory, you create the

\Images and \Documents subdirectories. So, if DNS is configured for
http://www.kirkland.net/ to point to the Web site, then users can also access files in
the http://www.kirkland. net/documents/ directory without any additional configuration in Internet Information Services. Of course, you can use NTFS security to
restrict this access, but that was covered in Chapter 3, "Integrating IIS with Windows
2000 Security," and Chapter 4, "IIS Security."

Virtual Directories

Although client browsers consider them identical, virtual directories have far more
capabilities than physical directories because they add an additional level of configuration. Virtual directories provide more flexibility in directory and file storage. They
can be used to present different directories, drives, and even servers as subdirectories
within a Web site. They also enable you to add storage capacity to your Web server
through the use of remote virtual directories without having to shut down the
server or add additional local hardware. The key to this extra configuration support
is the fact that when a virtual directory exists for a physical directory, the virtual
directory takes precedence.

Virtual directories can be created for folders located on the following:

- The same hard drive as the \InetPub directory
- Another hard drive inside the local computer
- Another hard drive on a remote computer across the network, which must be
  located within the same Windows 2000 domain as a local computer

One of the benefits of using virtual directories instead of physical directories is exem-
plified when you are using directories in an Intranet environment. For example, suppose that a company's internal Web site is located at http://Connectos/ on a physical
server in the MIS department. The Human Resources department maintains and
updates the company phone list on a server in the HR department. Instead of copying
the file to the MIS server and adding the complication of multiple versions of the
same document, it is simpler and more accessible for the phone list document to
remain on the server in the HR department. The Web server administrator needs only
to create a virtual directory named /Phonelist under the ConnectOS Web site. This
virtual directory points to the remote physical directory on the HR server. Now, the
phone list can be accessed from http://Connectos/Phonelist/.

Another key benefit to using virtual directories instead of physical directories is in
assigning security and permissions. The configuration information for a specific virtual directory takes precedence over the configuration information for the Web site.
For example, suppose that you create a Web site with only Read permissions. You then
create a virtual directory within the Web site that is configured with both read and
script permissions. Users accessing the virtual directory will be able to read files and
run scripts. Elsewhere in the Web site, users will have permission only to read files.

Yet another advantage of using a virtual directory is that it takes precedence if both a virtual directory and a physical directory share the same name. For example, suppose that you again create a Web site with only read permissions. Within the physical directory on the hard drive, you create the \Utilities subdirectory, which contains executable files. Because the Web site allows only read access, users cannot run the executables in the \Utilities directory. However, you can create a virtual directory that points to the physical directory and add execute permissions. When a user tries to access the \Utilities directory from a browser, Internet Information Services first determines if a virtual directory exists. Because it does, and is configured as described previously, IIS provides both read and execute access to the files.

If you are also using FrontPage to create and update your Web site, virtual directories create a unique situation. When looking at the Web site though FrontPage, you will not see any of the virtual directories. FrontPage will show you only physical directories within the Web site. However, the virtual directories do exist, so you can access them by specifically requesting one from FrontPage. This is the same issue with FTP and virtual directories discussed in Chapter 6, "Customizing the FTP Service."

Now that this chapter has covered the fundamentals of Web site functionality and organization, let's move on to some specific configuration options for Web sites in Internet Information Services 5. This chapter does not cover all the configuration options, but only those that are often misunderstood or new in Internet Information Services 5.

Operators

Every Web site on a single physical computer can be managed by the computer administrator. That is all most people reading this book need to know about operators. However, some of you will want to maintain general control of the system, while allowing someone else some administrative privileges to a specific Web site.

An account operator is a user who has limited administrative privileges for an individual Web site on a shared server. Account operators can administer properties that affect only their respective site; they do not have access to general properties of Internet Information Services or additional privileges in Windows 2000 Server. Use the Operators tab displayed in Figure 5.4 to add account operators for each individual Web site.

Virtual Directories Limitations

Internet Information Services allows for the creation of an almost unlimited number of virtual directories for each Web site. However, performance degradation will occur if you create too many because virtual directory configurations are stored in the metabase, and the metabase is stored in RAM. Use virtual directories only when required.

Figure 5.4   Specify Web site administrators on the Operators tab.

As a Web hosting provider, you can assign a Web administrator from each client company as an account operator for that Web site. The account operator can change or reconfigure the Web site as necessary, including setting Web site access permissions, enabling logging, changing the default document, setting content expiration, and enabling content ratings features. More importantly, though, is the configuration that the Web site operator is *not* permitted to change. The Web site operator cannot alter the identification of a Web site, including the configured IP address and port. This person also cannot configure security, including the anonymous username and password, and cannot make modifications that would be typically controlled by the server administrator, such as the amount of bandwidth available to the Web site.

In many hosting environments, though, even this limited amount of administrative privileges is too much to give to clients. Remember from previous chapters that you should give users only the permissions they need, and nothing more. If your clients need only to upload and download Web site files via FTP, then there is no reason to assign account operators for any site. The administrator can configure all options on all sites, and reconfiguration is rarely needed.

Home Directory

The next tab in the IIS snap-in for a specific Web site is actually the most important tab for a Web site. The Home Directory tab enables you to specify which physical directory is accessed when a user accesses the Web site. Recall that when a user types a URL, such as `http://www.connectos.com/`, a DNS server determines which IP address is referenced by the FQDN, and then the IIS server determines which physical directory is referenced by the IP address.

The home directory can be either local, remote, or a redirection to another URL. That is, the home directory can be a physical directory located on the Internet Information Services server, or the physical directory can be located on another computer in the same Windows 2000 domain as the IIS server. This is also true for a virtual directory, and, except for specific configuration, the information discussed here applies to both.

Local Directories

A local home directory is simple to configure. After selecting the option labeled "A directory located on this computer," as shown in Figure 5.5, you only need to type the correct path in the Local Path list box. However, because computers are very unforgiving to typographical errors, it is always safest to use the **Browse** button in order to ensure that you are referencing a valid physical directory.

Remote Directories

Configuring a remote home directory is a bit more complex. After you select the option labeled "A share located on another computer," new connection options appear. See Figure 5.6 to review the configuration requirements for a remote home directory.

The resulting options seem simple enough. First, identify the location of the remote data. Then identify the user context in which the data will be accessed. However, there are a lot of little issues here that will cause some big problems. The following absolute rules apply to remote directories:

Figure 5.5   A home directory that references a physical directory
on the same computer is said to be local.

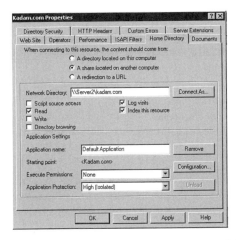

Figure 5.6   A home directory that references a physical directory on a different computer is said to be remote.

- The network directory must be typed as a Universal Naming Convention (UNC) address.
- The remote computer must be in the same Windows 2000 domain as the Internet Information Services server.
- The remote directory (share) must already be shared from Windows on the remote computer, or must be located within a shared directory.

After the correct server and share are specified, you must select the **Connect As. . .** button to enter the Windows 2000 account information that will be used to access the remote directory. After clicking the button, you are presented with the Network Directory Security Credentials dialog box requesting a username and password. You must type a valid Windows 2000 user account in the Username box in the form *DOMAIN\username*. You can also click the **Browse** button to receive a list of valid user accounts for the domain in which the Internet Information Services server resides or for a trusted domain. If you need a review of Windows 2000 domains and trust relationships, *Planning for Windows 2000*, by Eric Cone, Jon Boggs, and Sergio Perez, is a good resource (New Riders Publishing, 1999).

The username and password that you enter in the Network Directory Security Credentials dialog box is automatically used by every Web visitor who accesses data contained within the remote directory. I highly recommend that you create a Windows 2000 user account specifically for the purpose of remote connections. This user account should provide only the minimum permissions required to access the data and to effectively use the Web site. Any additional permissions are a potential security risk. And *never* (unless you really, really mean to) use the Windows 2000 administrator's account to access a remote directory. If you do this, you essentially will give a nonprivileged user administrative access to the remote resource. This is a bad thing.

Immediately after applying the configuration information for the remote directory, the Internet Information Services server logs on to the remote computer by using the username and password that you specified. This access to the remote directory remains constant for any and all users and is logged off only if the Web service is stopped for this Web site. It is then logged on again when the Web service is restarted. Internet Information Services makes this directory available as part of the Web site, appearing as a local physical directory. All users, whether anonymous or not, access the remote directory by using this username and password.

One last note on remote directories is that you may experience a decrease in Web site performance when accessing files and directories contained on another computer's hard drive. This performance drop is due to the transfer speed of data over a local area network (LAN).

URL Redirection

When you select "A redirection to a URL," the client can be sent to a URL specified or to a child directory. Most redirections are sent to another URL. For example, Internet Information Services could take all requests sent to `http://www.eastside.net/kirkland` to `http://www.kirkland.net/`. One reason to do this may be to use a portion of a Web site in multiple Web sites and have that portion appear as if it belongs to the original URL. You could also map a home directory to a child directory or a subdirectory.

One of the most flexible attributes of redirections in Internet Information Services 5 is the capability to use redirect variables. A redirect variable enables you to pass portions of the original URL with the destination URL. For example, you may want to redirect only the FQDN and ignore requests for specific subdirectories or files. On the other hand, you may want to redirect the full request, subdirectories and all, to another URL.

Host Headers

Each Web site must have a unique combination of IP address, TCP port, and host header name. For example, if you configure physical servers or virtual servers, each Web site is assigned a unique IP address. Or, you could assign a common IP address to

Local Directory Creation in IIS 4

In Internet Information Server 4, you cannot create a local physical directory from the **Browse** button in Microsoft Management Console. You should create the physical directory from Windows Explorer before configuring the Web site. You can configure the Web site first and then create the physical directory later; however, the Web site won't work until the physical directory is created.

all Web sites on a single Internet Information Services server and configure a unique TCP port to each Web site. Still another option is to configure all Web sites with a common IP address and common TCP port, and then assign each site a unique host header. By doing this, you can host multiple Web sites on a single Internet Information Services server using a single IP address and TCP port.

When a visitor types the FQDN for a target Web site into an HTTP 1.1-compliant Web browser, the browser includes the FQDN in the host header of the request to the server. IIS then routes the request to the virtual server configured with the identified IP address, TCP port, and host header. The visitor is then transferred transparently to the site requested.

Now that you've learned the basics of host headers, you can delve into a more technical discussion. This section begins with an overview of HTTP 1.1 and its features and benefits, and then discusses how to effectively implement a host header in Internet Information Services. Finally, it highlights both the advantages and disadvantages to consider before deciding whether to implement host headers. Review Figure 5.7 if you have not used host headers previously.

HTTP 1.1

Before jumping in to host headers, let's spend a short time on the protocol that makes it work: Hypertext Transfer Protocol version 1.1 (HTTP 1.1). When a Web client that supports HTTP 1.1 makes an HTTP request to a server, it identifies itself as an HTTP 1.1 client. Internet Information Services responds with an HTTP 1.1 transaction.

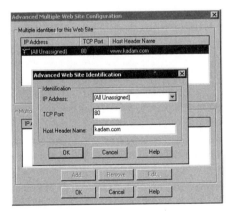

Figure 5.7   Internet Information Services supports multiple host headers for a single Web site.

Limitations of Host Headers

Only Web sites can take advantage of host headers. Internet Information Services cannot use them to distinguish services using protocols other than HTTP, including FTP and HTTPS (Web sites using SSL).

If the client supports only HTTP 1.0, IIS reverts to HTTP 1.0 and responds with a normal HTTP 1.0 transaction.

For a transaction to take advantage of the HTTP 1.1 protocol, both the Web server and the browser client must support it. Microsoft began implementing HTTP 1.1 in Internet Explorer 3.0, and Netscape began implementing it in Navigator 2.0.

Internet Information Server 4 and Internet Information Services 5 implement all the HTTP 1.1 features, including the following highlights:

- Persistent connections
- Pipelining
- HTTP PUT and HTTP DELETE

Persistent Connections

When a client connects to a Web server and requests an object, such as a Web page, the client establishes a connection with the server and downloads the object. Then the server drops the connection. However, an HTML page may contain multiple additional objects, such as images and sounds. Each object requires its own individual connection. So, a Web page with five graphics and one sound will require seven different connections in sequence to download and display that one page in a Web browser. These multiple connections require a lot of overhead for the client, server, and network.

By using persistent connections, or HTTP keepalives, HTTP 1.1-compliant browsers can remain connected to the Web server for a specified period without having to re-establish a connection to the server for each request. Both the client and the server must support HTTP keepalives. The client will send HTTP keepalives to tell the Web server not to drop the connection. The Web server must acknowledge this request to maintain a persistent connection until the client completes the download of all objects.

Pipelining

Generally, a client must wait for a response from the Web server for its request before it can send another request. In the example used in the "Persistent Connections" section, the client needed to download seven objects to view the entire Web page. The client would have had to wait for a response for each request before it submitted the next request.

Using pipelining, clients can send many requests before receiving a response from the Web server. You'll notice that if all requests are queued at once, the smaller objects download first. You have probably noticed that with Internet Explorer 4.0 and Internet Information Server 4 or later, the last object to appear on a Web page is usually the largest graphic. Pipelining provides HTTP 1.1-compliant browsers with a performance boost when accessing an Internet Information Server 4 or later Web site.

HTTP PUT and *HTTP DELETE*

HTTP 1.1 supports two new commands with a lot of potential. With HTTP PUT and HTTP DELETE, users can now post and delete files to and from a Web site by using the standard HTTP protocol. This makes HTTP a writable protocol. Of course, to utilize this new feature, you need to use a client that supports HTTP 1.1 and that provides a method for writing data. For a specific discussion on tools that make this available, see Chapter 8, "Microsoft FrontPage Server Extensions."

Adding Host Headers

As discussed earlier, the host header is used in combination with an IP address and a TCP port. Because of this relationship, host headers are configured in the same location as both the IP address and the TCP port for a particular Web site. Although a host header is a header used by the HTTP protocol, it is not—and cannot be—configured on the HTTP Header tab of the IIS-snap in of the Microsoft Management Console.

To configure the host header for a Web site after you have created the Web site, perform the following steps:

1. From Microsoft Management Console, right-click the Web site and select **Properties**.
2. On the Web Site tab, click the **Advanced** button in the Web Site Identification section.
3. In the Advanced Multiple Web Site Configuration dialog box, click the **Add** button in the Multiple Identities for This Web Site section.
4. Enter the IP address (or choose "All unassigned") in the IP Address box.
5. Enter the TCP port in the TCP Port box.
6. Enter the FQDN in the Host Header Name box.
7. Click **OK** to accept the changes.

In addition to configuring the host header information in Internet Information Services, you must also register the host header name and associated IP address with a DNS server before Web users will be able to access the new site. To register this information with a DNS server, follow the standard procedure of creating a zone file and appropriate resource (A) records. If you need more DNS information than what was covered in Chapter 3, then *DNS and BIND*, 2nd Edition, by Paul Albitz and Cricket Liu, (O'Reilly, 1998) is an excellent resource.

Pros and Cons to Using Host Headers

Originally, host headers seemed to be the perfect solution to small ISPs that wanted to host multiple Web sites but that had only one IP address to configure. However, the disadvantages of host headers quickly became as prevalent as their advantages. First, virtual servers that use host headers are accessible only by using an HTTP version 1.1-compliant Web browser. Without an HTTP version 1.1-compliant browser, any user attempting to access a Web site that uses host headers will instead receive the default Web site. Also, if the Web site configured with the requested host header is stopped, the user will receive the default Web site. For these reasons, host headers are not as prominent as originally anticipated.

Another problem with host headers is that Web sites that use them cannot support Secure Socket Layer (SSL). In this case, the host header is still encrypted at the point at which Internet Information Services needs to determine the certificate to use to unencrypt the data.

Host headers still have certain advantages, however. One benefit that Internet presence providers (IPP) receive by using host headers is that multiple virtual servers can be configured with a single IP address. An additional benefit to the IPP, although probably never mentioned, is that Web users without an HTTP version 1.1-compliant browser will most likely receive the IPP's Web site instead of receiving the requested Web site.

The issue with receiving the IPP's Web site stems from the requirement for HTTP 1.1-compliant Web browsers. Noncompliant browsers will request only the IP address, not the host header. And, because many sites will be using one IP address but be distinguished by the host header, noncompliant browsers will simply get one Web site associated with the IP address. Internet Information Services provides support for noncompliant browsers by optionally displaying a list of all Web sites associated with the IP address and allowing the user to select the one he wants. You could even go so far as passing a cookie to the user that identifies which Web site should be accessed during future requests. However, this solution will not allow a single Web user to access multiple sites associated with that one IP address.

The benefit that Web site customers receive from using host headers is reduced cost for Web hosting in a shared environment. However, as mentioned previously, the trade-off is that some users will be redirected from the attempted Web site to the IPP's Web site. Most IPPs that use host headers describe this process in their service description and provide a list of all Web hosting customers from their own Web site.

Server Extensions

Internet Information Services 5 introduced one new Web site configuration tab in the IIS snap-in of the Microsoft Management Console. The Server Extensions tab separates the configuration for a Web site that has been extended by using the Server Extensions of Microsoft FrontPage2000. *FrontPage Server Extensions* are a set of programs used to take full advantage of FrontPage2000. These programs can help manage, create, and view a FrontPage-extended Web site.

A check box at the top of this tab is used to enable authoring. When this box is checked, the FrontPage Extensions are enabled, including allowing a remote administrator to access and modify the selected Web site. Additional configuration on this tab affects mail options and security settings. Because of the complexity of the FrontPage Server Extensions, however, this tab will be covered in detail in Chapter 8. Refer to that chapter for information on the new options as well as screen shots and recommendations for effectively using the extensions.

6

Customizing the FTP Service

F ILE TRANSFER PROTOCOL (FTP) HAS BEEN a required protocol of the TCP/IP
Protocol stack since 1973. Microsoft first offered an FTP Server Service as a simple,
limited implementation in Windows NT 3.5. When Microsoft released Internet
Information Server 1 in 1995, the implementation was greatly enhanced but still
lacked several key features that were needed for a truly complete implementation. In
Internet Information Server 4, Microsoft made significant advances that finally allowed
it to support the features that would enable an Internet hosting provider to efficiently
commercialize its FTP services. Although Internet Information Services 5 adds few
additional advances, this version of the FTP service is a comprehensive solution for
almost all FTP scenarios.

This chapter covers the following topics:

- A brief review of FTP architecture
- Specific options configured on the FTP Site tab
- The three types of security accounts that can access an FTP site
- Specific options configured on the Home Directory tab
- A discussion of FTP virtual directories
- A step-by-step setup of an FTP site

FTP Architecture

TCP provides a connection-oriented service because FTP uses the Transmission Control Protocol (TCP) at the transport layer. All data exchanged between the server and the client is guaranteed to not only to be delivered, but also to be delivered intact as originally sent. Figure 6.1 diagrams the core functionality of FTP. If this diagram looks all too familiar, feel free to jump ahead to the next section. However, if it looks just vaguely familiar or not at all familiar, take the time to read through the section. Understanding the architecture of FTP not only helps with configuration now, but it also assists in troubleshooting later.

FTP not only uses TCP port 21 for session control, but it also uses port 20 for data transfer. When you first FTP to a site by typing, for example, ftp ftp.connectos.com, you enter into an interactive session with the FTP server. The FTP service on the server is listening on port 21—that is, any requests for that port were sent to the FTP service. You should now have a TCP connection from a client port on your local computer to TCP port 21 on the FTP server.

But if you decide to transfer a file, that will obviously require another port because TCP port 21 is already in use and only one service can use a port at any time. For example, if you type get test.txt at the FTP prompt, you will establish a second connection from another client port on your local computer to TCP port 20 on the FTP server computer. This works the same way when you upload a file to the server.

The following list of connections was obtained from the computer with IP address 209.67.75.69. Notice that the third connection is from the local client TCP port 1310 to the FTP server's TCP port 21. This was the establishment of the FTP session. The

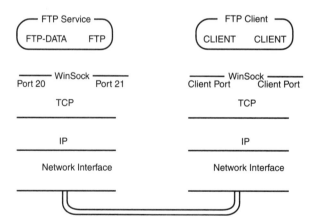

Figure 6.1   TCP is the core transport protocol of FTP.

last connection is from local TCP port 1313, a second client port, to the FTP server's port 20. This is the data transfer for a file.

```
C:\>netstat -n
Active Connections
   Proto  Local Address           Foreign Address         State
   TCP    127.0.0.1:1026          127.0.0.1:1031          ESTABLISHED
   TCP    127.0.0.1:1031          127.0.0.1:1026          ESTABLISHED
   TCP    209.67.73.69:1310       209.67.75.100:21        ESTABLISHED
   TCP    209.67.73.69:1312       209.67.75.100:139       ESTABLISHED
   TCP    209.67.73.69:1313       209.67.75.100:20        ESTABLISHED
C:\>
```

FTP Site Properties

You probably already have a lot of experience configuring the FTP Site tab in the Properties dialog box of the FTP virtual server, so this chapter covers only two of the configuration options on that page: IP Address and TCP Port. The IP Address option allows for FTP virtual servers, a configuration available only in Internet Information Server 4 and Internet Information Services 5. The TCP Port option allows for custom configuration not often used. Because of these capabilities, these topics warrant discussion in this book. If you need a review of the dialog box, see Figure 6.2.

IP Address

The capability to configure FTP virtual servers is one of the best features of the FTP service in Internet Information Services, first introduced in Internet Information Server 4. Most likely, you will configure one FTP virtual server for each WWW virtual server you have configured. As with WWW virtual servers, only one FTP virtual server can be configured with the IP address of All Unassigned, meaning that Internet

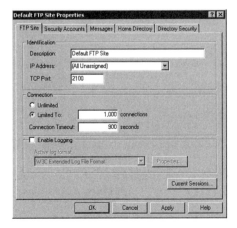

Figure 6.2 The IP Address and TCP Port options allow for FTP site customization and minimal security enhancements.

Information Services can support a single default FTP site for any IP address that is not specifically assigned to an individual FTP virtual server.

The All Unassigned option refers to all IP addresses configured in Windows 2000 that are not assigned to a specific FTP virtual server. If an IP address is assigned to a WWW virtual server but not to an FTP virtual server, then it is still unassigned for the FTP service and will be a part of the All Unassigned category when configured for another FTP virtual server.

TCP Port

FTP listens on TCP port 21 by default, but you can change the port for the FTP service. There are two places where you can change the listening port:

- The `Services` file located in the *winnt_root*`\system32\drivers\etc` directory
- The Internet Information Services metabase

Changing the listening port really does one thing: It provides for a bit of very rudimentary security. If a user on the Internet knows your Web address and wants to get into your file list, then that person may guess that he can use the FTP protocol to access the same data. Most FTP clients request TCP port 21 when trying to access the data. If you change the FTP listening port, you've eliminated the wild guesses. However, anyone with a port scanner could determine the new listening port in a just few minutes.

The *Services* File

The `Services` file that ships with previous versions of Windows NT and Windows 2000 includes the following two lines:

```
ftp-data          20/tcp
ftp               21/tcp
```

These lines indicate that all FTP clients will request TCP port 21 by default, and all FTP services will listen on TCP port 21 by default. You can easily change the default for both FTP clients and FTP services by editing the `Services` file. The `Services` file must then be saved in the same directory, and it cannot have a file extension.

The Internet Information Services Metabase

If you want to change only the FTP listening port for all FTP clients, not the requesting port, you must change the port in the Internet Information Services Metabase. Or, if you want to change the FTP listening port for an individual FTP site, you need to change the port in the Internet Information Services Metabase. Recall that the Metabase stores configuration information for Internet Information Services and all its virtual servers and virtual directories. To change the FTP listening port in the Metabase, use the FTP Site tab of the FTP Site Properties dialog box.

Additional Notes

Recall that in Internet Information Server 3, no Internet Information Services Metabase exists. All configuration information was stored in the NT Registry. Also, Internet Information Server 3 didn't support FTP virtual servers, so you really only had one FTP site. In Internet Information Server 3, if the NT Registry was configured with a different FTP listening port than the Services file, the FTP listening port used by the FTP site was the one that had been configured in the NT Registry.

In Internet Information Server 4 and Internet Information Services 5.0, if the Internet Information Services Metabase is configured with a different FTP listening port than is configured in the Services file, then the FTP listening port used by a specific FTP site is the one configured in the Internet Information Services Metabase. For example, suppose that the FTP port is configured for port 21 in the Services file. You then use the IIS snap-in (to the MMC) to configure the FTP port for your own Web site to port 2100. When the FTP service starts for your FTP site, it listens on port 2100.

Because the Metabase overrides the Services file, you have the opportunity to configure a different FTP listening port on each individual FTP site. So, instead of requiring multiple IP addresses for multiple FTP sites, you can use one IP address and multiple listening ports for the FTP service. If you are limited in the number of IP addresses available to you, this enables you to configure and host multiple FTP sites.

Security Accounts

Again, security is the single most important aspect of configuring any server that is accessible to tens of thousands of users. Early chapters discussed the planning of a secure server and touched on many of the configuration options available for the FTP service. This section now summarizes and clarifies the options specific to the FTP service in Internet Information Services 5. For a quick review of the Security Accounts property sheet, see Figure 6.3.

Figure 6.3   New in Windows 2000, the default anonymous FTP account is different than the default anonymous Web account.

Anonymous Users

Recall that two distinct classes of users can access Internet Information Services: anonymous users and nonanonymous users. By default, Internet Information Services prefers users to access the FTP service by using the anonymous account. By default, anonymous users are represented to Windows 2000 security as the IUSR_*computername* account for both the WWW service and the FTP service.

Unfortunately, the roles of the WWW service and the FTP service are very different. As such, the security required for each is also different. To better distinguish between the two services, both for security and for auditing purposes, you should create a separate anonymous user account for the WWW service and the FTP service.

In our company's case, we changed the anonymous username for all FTP sites to IUSR_FTP. We can now configure anonymous access separately for WWW users and FTP users. This was also the best configuration in previous versions of Internet Information Server.

However, with the implementation of FTP virtual servers in Internet Information Server 4, you could take security one step further: You could create a separate anonymous user account for each FTP virtual server. If this is necessary in your environment, then you can and should create multiple accounts. For example, if you need to implement security auditing for anonymous users from individual FTP sites, you will need to create multiple anonymous FTP accounts. In most cases, however, anonymous users are anonymous users, so there's no need to distinguish among them individually.

The check box for "Allow only anonymous connections" is a more restrictive version of the check box for "Allow anonymous connections." Both control the scope of security accounts available to you as the administrator. Although checking both boxes is the most restrictive environment for the administrator, it is also the most secure environment. If you remove the check from either option, you will receive the warning message shown in Figure 6.4. With the nonanonymous connection, you deal with a whole new set of issues.

Nonanonymous Users

As indicated by the previous error message, Microsoft generally does not recommend nonanonymous connections to the FTP service. When a user logs on to the FTP

Figure 6.4   Because FTP transfers all passwords as clear text,
anonymous connections are the most secure.

service, that user must supply a username and password. These credentials are passed to the Windows 2000 security subsystem for validation. The issue is that both are transmitted as *clear text*, meaning without encryption, from the user's location to the server. In the case of a valid nonanonymous connection, this means that a valid Windows 2000 user account and password are transferred across the Internet. Although this is certainly a security concern, security risks can be reduced—and even eliminated—with proper planning and configuration of NTFS security. Using NTFS security, reduce the amount of access that each account has to only those resources that it needs.

However, there are several extremely valid reasons to allow nonanonymous connections. For example, if your users require FTP to upload files to their Web sites, you almost have no option but to allow nonanonymous FTP. You don't want most users to upload files, but you'll need to allow the Web site designer to do so. To allow all users to download files via FTP but only one user to upload files via FTP, you must be able to distinguish among users, and this must be done with nonanonymous FTP.

Each nonanonymous account that you configure for FTP access must be given the Windows 2000 permission for "Log on Locally." In pure Windows 2000 terms, this means that the user account can log on interactively with the local computer. In the case of FTP, the FTP service logs on interactively with the local computer by using the designated Windows 2000 account. Although this would make almost any administrator nervous, there should be no way for an Internet user to actually gain physical access to the computer running Internet Information Services. So, although technically there is a security risk, it is minimal.

To simplify administration of Windows 2000 accounts used for FTP access, our company created a local Windows 2000 group called FTP Admins. We then granted this group the right to log on locally. As we create new Windows 2000 accounts for nonanonymous FTP access, we add each user account to this group. They now have appropriate rights, and we can track all the FTP accounts as a single administrative entity.

Account Synchronization

Next to the capability to configure FTP virtual servers, the check box for "Enable automatic password synchronization" was the best new feature of the FTP service in Internet Information Server 4. This same feature is now labeled "Allow IIS to control password" in Internet Information Services 5. When the check box is selected, the Password box becomes disabled. Any changes made in Active Directory Computers and Users to the password of the account listed in the Username box are automatically reflected in the FTP service. This enables you to keep up with the password in only one location. You may also be interested to know that the functionality is the same as it was in previous versions of Internet Information Server—the service simply ignores the password. Of course, this is no less secure than one service copying the password from another server on the same computer.

Home Directory

The last FTP property sheet discussed here is on the Home Directory tab. Each FTP site requires a *home directory*. When a user connects to an FTP site, that user lands in the physical directory designated as the FTP site directory on the Home Directory tab of the Home Directory properties sheet. See Figure 6.5 if you need to review this property sheet.

This section discusses the difference between local and remote directories, types of access to the FTP site, and directory listing styles.

Local versus Remote

The FTP site directory can either be local or remote. If local, the physical directory exists on the same computer as Internet Information Services and is identified by selecting the radio button for **A directory located on this computer**. If remote, the physical directory exists on a different computer, either on the same subnet or on a remote subnet, and is identified by selecting the radio button **For a share located on another computer**.

As simple as it is to configure local directories, it can be just as complex to configure remote directories. After it's indicated that the FTP home directory is located on a remote computer, new options will appear on the Home Directory property sheet. Notice the changes to Home Directory tab, as indicated in Figure 6.6.

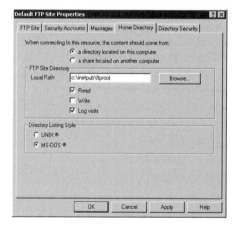

Figure 6.5   FTP sites are associated with a physical directory
on the Home Directory property sheet.

Asterisks in the Password Box

Internet Information Services 5 always displays 10 asterisks in the Password box, regardless of the number of characters in the password. User Manager always displays 14 asterisks. However, with Internet Information Server versions 3 and 4, the asterisks displayed in the Password box actually represented the number of characters in the password. Good change, Microsoft.

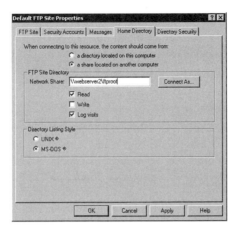

Figure 6.6 Remote virtual directories require a URL to locate
it and an account to connect with.

The FTP service attaches to remote directories by using a standard NetBIOS connection. The remote computer can be running Windows NT, Windows 2000, Windows
9x, or even SAMBA on Linux. Because of the NetBIOS connection, the computer
running the FTP service must have the Workstation service enabled, and the remote
computer with the physical directory must have the Server service enabled.
Additionally, the remote physical directory must be *shared* from the remote computer,
and appropriate permissions must be configured on both the share and within NTFS.

So what are appropriate permissions? The two options that are unique to a remote
home directory are a Network Share box and a **Connect As**. . . button. The
computer running the FTP service will connect to the remote home directory by
using this Windows 2000 account and the remote share. So, you must configure this
Windows 2000 account with a minimum of read permissions both in NTFS and on
the share. Figure 6.7 displays results of the **Connect As**. . . button.

Any access to the data in the remote home directory is granted to the Windows
2000 account specified in the **Connect As**. . . dialog box. Because the connection is

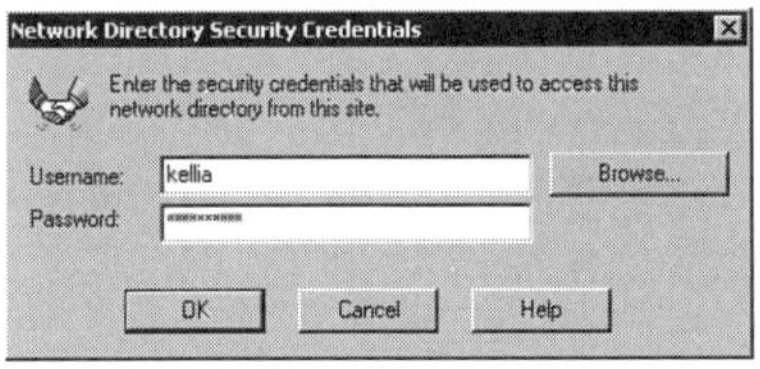

Figure 6.7 The FTP server must log in to a computer
that contains a remote directory.

established only once, when the FTP service is started for the site, all access to this directory is in the context of the specified user. So, NTFS cannot be used to configure different permissions for different users. Figure 6.8 diagrams the logical connection from the FTP server computer to a computer that houses a remote directory.

Access Permissions

The directory permissions assigned from the Home Directory tab of the FTP site property sheet apply to *every* connection made to the FTP site. This includes both anonymous and nonanonymous connections. So, suppose that you want most users to connect to an FTP site with an anonymous connection and obtain read permissions, but you need the Web master to FTP to the site as a nonanonymous user and obtain both read and write access. In this case, you must select both the "Read" and "Write" check boxes.

The problem with this scenario is that now *all* connections will obtain read and write permissions to the directory. How do you secure the files from the anonymous users? With NTFS permissions! You could configure the NTFS permissions for the Web master's nonanonymous account to change, and the NTFS permissions for the anonymous user account to read.

Directory Listing Style

It might seem surprising that Microsoft, the maker of MS-DOS, defaults to the UNIX directory style listing. Well, it shouldn't surprise you. For years, the predominant operating system on the Internet was UNIX. So, if you want your FTP directory listing to be readable by the widest range of clients, leave the directory listing style as UNIX.

However, the MS-DOS directory style listing does, offer some advantages. It provides more information than the UNIX directory listing. The tradeoff is that MS-DOS listing supports only 8.3 filenames.

Whether you use the UNIX or MS-DOS directory style listing, visitors to your site can generate a directory listing by typing either ls or dir at the FTP prompt.

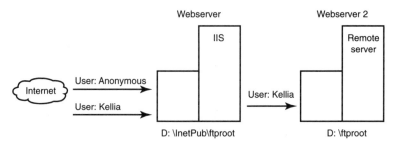

Figure 6.8 The FTP service requires a user context to log
on to a computer housing a remote directory.

The `ls` command generates a simple list of files and directories, as follows:

```
ftp> ls
200 PORT command successful.
150 Opening ASCII mode data connection for file list.
chapter3.doc
new_util.zip
technote.doc
226 Transfer complete.
43 bytes received in 0.01 seconds (4.30 Kbytes/sec)
```

The `dir` command generates a more detailed list:

```
ftp> dir
200 PORT command successful.
150 Opening ASCII mode data connection for /bin/ls.
-rwxrwxrwx   1 owner     group          279449 Mar 31  8:28 chapter3.doc
-rwxrwxrwx   1 owner     group         1960359 Oct 21  1997 new_util.zip
-rwxrwxrwx   1 owner     group            3333 May  5 17:05 technote.doc
226 Transfer complete.
220 bytes received in 0.03 seconds (7.33 Kbytes/sec)
```

The most important thing to note is that only physical files and directories are contained in the list. *Physical* files and directories exist within the FTP site directory on the hard drive, either as files or as subdirectories. In contrast, *virtual* directories exist either within a different directory on the hard drive or on another server altogether. Virtual directories are configured by adding new virtual directories to the current FTP virtual server.

FTP Virtual Directories

The most important characteristic of FTP virtual directories is that they do not appear in directory lists unless specifically configured to do so. Another characteristic to note is that, like FTP home directories described previously, FTP remote virtual directories are accessed by a single Windows 2000 account, which must have permissions granted to it for both the share and in NTFS.

However, there is a way to work around some of these issues. You can use multiple remote directories to separate permissions. This is not a very efficient or very secure method, though. For example, from the FTP site `ftp.connectos.com`, suppose that I create two remote virtual directories. One is called *private*, and the other is called *public*. Both use the same Windows 2000 account to access the same remote physical directory. However, the private virtual directory is configured with both read and write permissions, while the public virtual directory is configured with only read permissions. Because neither appears in the directory list, users could be told about, or linked to, the public virtual directory, but only the Web designer is told about the private virtual directory. Still, if a user finds out or guesses the location of the private virtual directory, then he also can change the files.

Step-by-Step Setup

Although FTP can be a simple service, it can be complex in certain environments. The following general steps highlight the steps that can be required to set up a secured FTP site:

1. Create Windows 2000 user accounts for nonanonymous users who will access the FTP site.

2. Create the physical directory for the FTP site on the local computer.

3. Configure NTFS permissions on the physical directory.

4. Create the new FTP site by using the Microsoft Management Console.

5. Modify the security accounts and other configuration information, if desired.

6. Start the FTP service for the new site.

This chapter primarily focused on step five, configuring the FTP site. For more information on configuring and integrating security, refer to Chapter 3 "Integrating IIS with Windows 2000 Security," and Chapter 4, "IIS Security." For more information on some of the general service information discussed here, such as accounts and directories, see Chapter 5 "Customizing WWW Sites." If you are looking for a detailed discussion of the entire setup process, I recommend the online help. As with any technical topic, however, the best education is experience, so just create an FTP site and work with it.

7

Running Web Applications

ALTHOUGH THE MAJORITY OF WEB SITES today contain static content—that is, standard HTML pages—many companies are finding that it takes something a little more exciting to attract, keep, and provide value to their customers. Web applications allow Webmasters to pull information from databases, accept product orders online, personalize pages for individual users, and provide a myriad of other services to their users. As an Internet Information Services administrator, you will need to enable these applications for your clients and possibly even educate your clients a bit on their value. This chapter provides you with the information you will need to complete these tasks; however, it does not teach you how to create Web applications or code within Web pages. You might find that helpful, or maybe even necessary, in your specific job, but it is not something that the normal Internet Information Services administrator will need to know. For that reason, this topic isn't covered here.

The Web applications discussed in this chapter are executed and processed on the Web server. These applications are different from client-side executables. The advantages of server-side applications over client-side applications include browser independence, better bandwidth utilization, and logged application errors. With client-side applications, none of these are available.

The chapter covers the following topics:

- An overview of Web applications running on Internet Information Services
- MIME types and how they are configured

- ISAPI applications
- ASP applications
- How to load and configure a Web application in Internet Information Services

Applications and Internet Information Services

A *Web application* could be a script within a single ASP page, a Java applet, or a custom application encompassing hundreds of Web pages. A given Web site can contain more than one Web application. Multiple Web applications are distinguished by the application's *starting-point directory*, or root directory, within the Web site. All the content within this directory and the directories below it are considered to be part of the Web application until another application starting point is encountered.

Server Development Technologies

Internet Information Services support multiple types of Web applications, including ASP, ISAPI, CGI, IDC, and SSI. Historically, the most common types of applications were Common Gateway Interface (CGI) applications and Perl scripts. Both of these technologies were created for use on UNIX-based Web servers. It wasn't until Microsoft created Internet Information Server in 1996 that these technologies became popular on a Windows NT computer and now on a Windows 2000 server.

As Internet Information Services has matured, so have the application technologies that it supports. With Internet Information Server, Microsoft introduced a new Web-based application technology called Internet Services Application Programming Interface (ISAPI). ISAPI (pronounced "I-sapi") was created exclusively for use on an Internet Information Services server. Then, with Internet Information Server 3, Microsoft introduced yet another technology called Active Server Pages (ASP). Today, ASP is the most widely used application technology on Internet Information Services 5.

Generally, the different applications can be distinguished by their file types, or file extensions. As a Web administrator, you will probably not be developing Web applications, but you will want to have a general knowledge of which type of applications your clients are running on your Web server. Following are the applications and their most common file extensions:

Application Type	Common Extension
CGI	.exe
Perl	.pl
ISAPI	.dll
ASP	.asp

Global versus Per Site Configuration

Most of the configuration discussed in this chapter can be configured either for an individual Web site or for all Web sites on the Internet Information Services server. To configure an individual Web site, simply right-click the Web site name within the Internet Information Services snap-in in the Microsoft Management Console (MMC), and then click **Properties**. Any configurations made within the properties of the individual site affect only that site.

To configure all Web sites at once, configure the master property sheets of the Internet Information Services server. To do this, right-click the computer name in the Internet Information Services snap-in, select **WWW Service** in the Master Properties list box, and click **Edit**. But, let me give you one note of warning here: If you configure an individual Web site, add a MIME mapping, and then configure and reapply the master properties, Internet Information Services will replace the individual site properties with the new master properties.

Web Application Manager (WAM)

Beginning with Internet Information Server 4, applications in Internet Information Services are processed by the Web Application Manager (WAM) that runs with Microsoft Transaction Server. This architecture of Internet Information Services was designed to provide a high level of performance for static, dynamic, and Web application content, while maintaining the reliability of Internet Information Services when running Web applications. Because static content doesn't affect the reliability of the Web server, all static requests are serviced immediately by InetInfo. This improves the performance of static content.

On the other hand, Web applications can run either in process or out of process. The definition of and difference between these states will be discussed in Chapter 13, "Performance Tuning and Reliability." Because of this flexibility, Web applications are managed by an internal object called the WAM. WAM itself is a Common Object Model (COM) component registered with Microsoft Transaction Server (MTS) and can be run in process or out of process. MTS, which is a run-time environment for COM components, hosts a WAM proxy object for each isolated process. Figure 7.1 shows how the WAM processes Web applications in Internet Information Services.

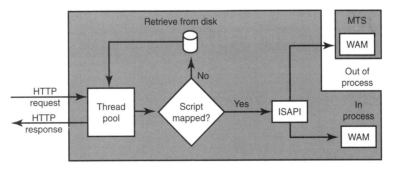

Figure 7.1   Internet Information Services creates one WAM for all in-process applications, one for the pooled applications, and individual WAMs for each out-of-process application.

When Internet Information Services receives a request for a Web application, the WAM determines whether the Web application is configured to run out of process. If so, the WAM forwards the request to an external MTS process. Otherwise, the request is completed in process with Internet Information Services. The WAM hosts all Web applications, whether they're in process or not, and controls loading and interfacing with ISAPI DLLs. During the installation of Internet Information Services, the IWAM_computername account is created. This is the Internet Information Services Web Application Manager identity and is used to start out-of-process Web applications in Internet Information Services.

Configuring MIME Types

Multipurpose Internet Mail Extension (MIME) mapping provides a way of configuring browsers to view files that are in multiple formats. MIME mapping is an extension of the Internet mail protocol that allows any file type hosted on an Internet Information Services server to be opened by a "helper" application on Web clients. Internet Information Services installs the most common MIME types by default. MIME types for new applications or applications that are not widely used will have to be added manually. In some cases, a helper application may have to be configured on the Web client as well.

If your server provides files that are in multiple formats, it must have a MIME mapping for each file type. If MIME mapping on the server is not set up for a specific file type, Web clients may not be capable of retrieving the file correctly. Internet Information Services 5 contains a comprehensive list of MIME types. However, you might need to add additional MIME types to the MIME type list. To view MIME types specified by default in Internet Information Services, right-click a Web site, choose **Properties**, and then select the **HTTP Headers** tab. On the HTTP Header tab, click the **File Types** button in the MIME Map section.

Some documents or applications might require a MIME type other than the default of text/html. To add a new MIME type, access the File Types dialog box described previously. Click the **New Type** button and add the appropriate files extension to the Associated Extension text box and the application mapping to the Content Type (MIME) text box. After you've done this, the new MIME mapping will appear in the Registered File Types list. For example, to allow your Web server to host .asx files for Windows Media Technologies content, input asx into the Associated Extension text box, and type video/x-ms-asf into the Content Type (MIME) text box.

ISAPI Applications

The Internet Server Application Programming Interface (ISAPI) provides an open specification that other software can use to control and interact with Internet

Information Services. Through ISAPI, an application can receive a Web client's request for a file, plus information that describes the client browser and connection to the Internet. Or, through ISAPI, an application can create a stream of data and send it to the Web server, which will then pass it to the client browser in a form similar to the contents of a normal HTML file. This action of creating returned data streams from an application is called *dynamic content*. *Static content*, in contrast, is simply HTML text.

The single most prominent disadvantage to ISAPI is that you need to be a full-fledged developer to write a component. Of course, for the developer, this is not a problem at all. However, most Web developers are exceptionally proficient in HTML, but probably not in C++. Microsoft might have realized this concern, or might have just been moving in the right direction at the right time, but shortly after ISAPI was introduced, a simpler solution came along.

ASP Applications

In response to the need for nonprogrammers to program Web sites, Microsoft introduced a new programming option, of sorts, in Internet Information Server 3. Active Server Pages (ASP) offered a relatively simple and inexpensive solution for dynamic and database-driven Web sites. To many, though, its biggest advantage is that it is simple to learn, especially for those Web designers familiar with Visual Basic.

Internet Information Services 5 includes ASP 3.0, a server-side scripting technology for building dynamic Web sites. ASP is basically just a text file, just like any HTML page. Internet Information Services is capable of distinguishing it and thus processing it because the text file has the extension `.asp`. A Web page with an `.asp` extension can contain plain HTML code, an active server component (or standard COM object), scripts, and references to ASP objects.

The two most common scripting languages used by ASP programmers are VBScript and JScript. VBScript is based on the Visual Basic programming language created by Microsoft in 1991. If a Web programmer can code Visual Basic, he will find VBScript very easy to pick up. Jscript, a scripting language created by Microsoft, is based on JavaScript programming language offered by Sun Microsystems. It is important to note, for political reasons as well as technical reasons, that JScript and Java are fundamentally different technologies. Other ASP scripting languages include PerlScript, Python, and Rexx.

When a Web client requests an `.asp` page from the Web server, Internet Information Services recognizes its format and begins processing it. Internet Information Services accesses any COM objects called in the Web page and parses any scripts coded in the page by sending the page to the ASP Scripting engine. The scripting host, located in `asp.dll`, checks the `global.asa` file for preprocessing instructions and then executes the server-side scripting code. Finally, the scripting host returns an HTML page to Internet Information Services, which in turn returns the HTML page to the requesting Web client. Figure 7.2 shows a diagram of ASP functionality in Internet Information Services.

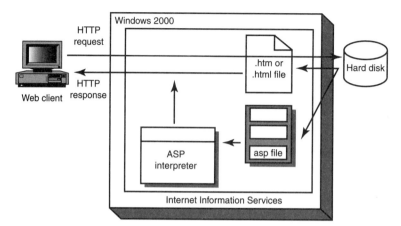

Figure 7.2   ASP pages are processed by Internet Information
Services before returning a static HTML page to the client.

Because ASP supports more than one scripting language, the ASP code must specify
which type of code it contains. This way, Internet Information Services can utilize the
correct interpreter. For example, the following line within an .asp file indicates the
beginning of a VBScript:

```
<%@ LANGUAGE= "VBScript" %>
```

Each Web application has its own set of variables and attributes that define its current
state. These variables are maintained as long as the application is active.

Enabling ASP

By default, ASP is enabled for all Web sites on an Internet Information Services server.
To test that ASP is running correctly on the server, simply launch the Internet
Information Services 5 documentation. If the documentation works, then ASP is run-
ning, because the documentation is entirely written in ASP.

Pros and Cons of ASP

Because you are running Internet Information Services on a Windows NT computer,
ASP is the best choice for use in creating dynamic Web sites. It's simple, it's easy to
learn, and it's free. It's also more efficient and easier to program than ISAPI.

> *Global.asa* **File**
>
> A Global.asa file stores information used globally by a Web application. A Global.asa file does not
> generate content that is displayed to Web user. Global.asa files contain only the following: application
> events, session events, object declarations, and type library declarations.
>
> Each Web site should use only one Global.asa file that must be stored in the starting point of the Web
> application. You must also provide read permissions on the Global.asa file for any Web user that will
> execute the Web application.

On the other hand, ASP can run a little slower than a compiled Perl script and doesn't have the entrenched following that most UNIX languages boast. It's even a bit slower than a static HTML page, though that is probably expected. But as mentioned in Chapter 13, just changing the extension of a file from `.htm` to `.asp` will cause it to load a bit slower. Finally, although this isn't confined to ASP or even all ASPs, running server-side scripts uses up resources and processing power on your server instead of offloading it to a client computer. The inherent dangers in reduced performance and reduced security should at least earn your consideration.

Creating a Web Application

Creating a Web application within Internet Information Services is as simple as designating the application's starting-point directory from within the IIS snap-in (to the MMC). When it's created, the MMC indicates a Web application by placing a package icon next to the directory name.

Of course, you can do a lot more to customize the application for your requirements. You can configure a Web application from the Home Directory tab of the Web site property sheet. After choosing an application name and designating the starting point, you're ready to set the properties for the application. Figure 7.3 displays the application settings options for enabling scripting within a Web site.

Most of the configuration discussed in the remainder of this section is completely optional, and you probably will not ever need to use it. As a good practice, however, you should give some thought to the effect of the Execute Permissions and the Application Protection drop-down boxes.

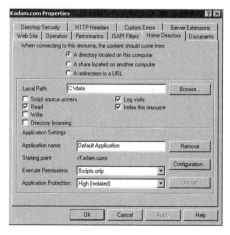

Figure 7.3   Create a Web application by configuring the application settings on the Home Directory property sheet.

Internet Information Services 5 provides you with three options in the Execute Permissions drop-down list: None, Scripts Only, and Scripts and Executables:

- **None.** Specifies that no script or application can be called from within the Web site.

- **Scripts Only.** Supports ASP code, such as VBScript and Jscript only. In this case, code can be embedded into a Web page, but pages cannot call ISAPI or CGI applications.

- **Scripts and Executables.** Allows all scripts also enabled with Scripts Only, plus executable files and DLLs. Although this option provides a Web programmer the most flexibility, it also provides the Web administrator with a bit of concern. Not only can a "bad" application cause problems for your Web server, but so can a "bad" programmer. They can now have the flexibility of running any script or program that they choose on your Web server and within its memory space and security context. Just be sure that you trust the Web programmer first.

Application Protection provides a nice level of security against those bad applications, but not against a bad programmer. In this case, Application Protection refers to shielding the Web server and other applications from an application that has failed. A detailed discussion of this configuration option can be found in Chapter 13.

When the Web application has been configured, you can further control the application by removing subdirectories from the application and by loading it to, or unloading it from, memory. All these actions are available through the use of buttons that appear within the Properties dialog box. Note, though, that the application can be loaded and unloaded only from its root directory; otherwise, the button is dimmed.

Selecting the **Configuration** button produces the Application Configuration dialog box with three tabs: App Mappings, App Options, and App Debugging.

App Mappings

The App Mappings property sheet is used to map filename extensions to the program that processes the files. This is applicable to ISAPI files, ASP files, IDC files, and other files that use server-side includes. For example, when a Web client requests an ASP file, the configured application mappings tell Internet Information Services to call `asp.dll` to process that page. Figure 7.4 displays the App Mappings property sheet.

Enabling the "Cache ISAPI Applications" check box tells Internet Information Services to cache API DLLs so that further applications can be run without again calling the program that processes the application. The check box is enabled by default and should stay that way unless it specifically needs to be disabled for testing purposes. Also, the check box will then need to be disabled for all applications that use that program; otherwise, Internet Information Services will not unload the program from memory.

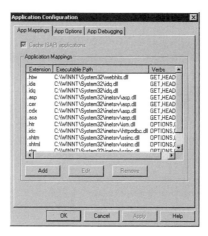

Figure 7.4   The App Mappings property sheet maps application file extensions to the program that will process those files.

App Options

You can use the App Options property sheet to control how ASP scripts are run within the application. These defaults generally work for all ASP applications, but you may want to customize them for your environment. The default settings shown in the App Options property sheet (displayed in Figure 7.5) ease a little of the coding required by a Web developer.

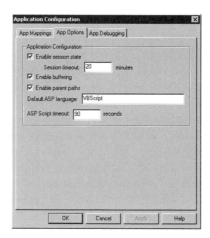

Figure 7.5   The App Options property sheet gives you several options to configure how an ASP script is run.

Application Configuration displays three check boxes:

- **Enable session state.** Causes ASP to create a session for each user who accesses an ASP application. With this enabled, Web programmers can track users across ASP pages in the Web site and store information in the Session object. The user session expires when the user does not request another ASP page within the specified timeout period.

- **Enable buffering.** Tells Internet Information Services to collect all output created by an ASP page before delivering it to the Web client. Enabling this check box allows the Web programmer to set HTTP headers from anywhere within the ASP script.

- **Enable parent paths.** Allows the Web programmer to use relative paths in ASP scripts. This makes programming a bit simpler but may allow the Web programmer to run an unauthorized application from the parent directory. If you want to tighten security for running applications on your Internet Information Services server, then clear this check box.

Application Configuration also displays two text boxes. The "Default ASP language" check box indicates the ActiveX script engine used to process ASP pages by default. Here you can specify any language for which an ActiveX script engine is installed on the Internet Information Services server. The "ASP Script timeout" text box specifies the amount of time, in seconds, that ASP will allow a script to run before stopping the script.

   More information on any of these options can be found in any standard ASP reference manual. For the Web programmer, all the options you select here, except for the "Enable parent paths" check box, can be overridden in the actual ASP script.

App Debugging

The App Debugging property sheet can be used to either help debug scripts or to inform Web clients what to do when a script error occurs. Unless your Web developer intends to analyze the information you gather, however, application debugging is something you will probably never use. One of the most underutilized features of Internet Information Services 5 is the capability to send custom ASP error messages to Web clients by configuring the App Debugging property sheet, as displayed in Figure 7.6. You may, however, choose to send a clear message to your Web clients in the event of a script error. By default, Internet Information Services will send the Web client the detailed ASP error—not very useful to most. You instead could say something like, "Oops! Please call us and we'll have someone look at this problem, and probably even fix it."

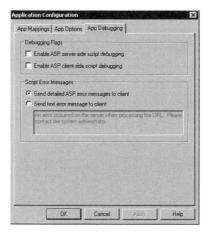

Figure 7.6   The App Debugging property sheet enables you to send informative messages to Web clients when a Web application fails.

The technologies described in this chapter enable a Web developer of any level to create dynamic, functional Web applications. However, those Web designers who are not Web developers would also like to create exciting Web sites. The next chapter discusses one method of doing this: by using Microsoft FrontPage.

8

Microsoft FrontPage
Server Extensions

ALTHOUGH MORE THAN 90% OF WEB SITES do not use Microsoft FrontPage Server Extensions, as an IIS administrator you are bound to have some clients who want the functionality that FrontPage provides. For those few clients, you need to know how the FrontPage Server Extensions work, how users connect to Web sites by using FrontPage, and what changes the FrontPage Server Extensions make to a Web server. This chapter provides that information.

Microsoft FrontPage is a robust Web site creation tool that requires little to no programming or even HTML experience. FrontPage includes features, such as wizards, graphical themes, templates, and active page elements, that make it easy for users to include complex functionality without programming. The FrontPage Server Extensions are a set of programs installed on the Web server. These programs provide portions of FrontPage's functionality, including setting separate permissions on sub-webs, easily incorporating database queries, and providing better support for third party snap-ins and utilities.

This chapter covers the following information:

- How to install the Microsoft FrontPage 2000 Server Extensions on an IIS
- How to effectively configure the FrontPage Server Extensions
- Options for administering the FrontPage Server Extensions
- Security configuration with FrontPage Server Extensions
- How FrontPage administrators connect to a FrontPage Web
- How FrontPage Server Extensions integrate with other services

Installing FrontPage 2000 Server Extensions

Before you can implement or configure FrontPage Webs on your Internet Information Services server, the Server Extensions must be installed. The following sections discuss the installation options and the changes that must be made to the system before you can install the Extensions.

The FrontPage 2000 Server Extensions are backward-compatible, meaning that clients using FrontPage 98 software will still have all the functionality that they had with the FrontPage 98 Server Extensions. However, the opposite is not true—a FrontPage 2000 client will lose some of the functionality if the server is using FrontPage 98 Server Extensions. Because of this, only the FrontPage 2000 Server Extensions should be installed for new Web sites, without considering the version of FrontPage that they are using on their client to create and modify the Web site.

Installation Overview

Before installing the FrontPage 2000 Server Extensions, you must first log on to Windows NT or Windows 2000 by using an administrator account. This level of permissions is required to install the FrontPage 2000 Server Extensions on the Web server, as well as on an individual virtual server. The Server Extensions and all related programs and files are copied to the Web server when you first install the Server Extensions to the Web server. If only one Web site exists on the Web server, then the extensions are automatically copied into the site directory.

After the Server Extensions have been installed on the Web server, you will then need to use the Internet Information Services snap-in (to the Microsoft Management Console) to add the Server Extensions to each individual virtual server if more than one virtual server exists on the Web server. See the section "Configuring FrontPage 2000 Extensions" later in this chapter, for a detailed description.

To install the FrontPage 2000 Server Extensions, run the `servext.exe` file. The location of this file depends on which method you use to install. The FrontPage 2000 Server Extensions are free and can be found on Microsoft's Web site at `http://msdn.microsoft.com/workshop/c-frame.htm?934215889682#/workshop/languages/fp/`. They are also included with all retail versions of FrontPage 2000. If you install from the FrontPage 2000 Server Extensions CD, the program is located at `X:\windows\servext.exe`, where `X` is the drive letter for your CD-ROM.

During installation, the Server Extensions are copied to the following folder:

```
C:\Program Files\Common Files\Microsoft Shared\Web Server Extensions\40\Bin
```

Extensions to Other Software

The FrontPage 2000 Server Extensions are also used to support other Web development software, including Microsoft Visual InterDev.

and

`C:\Program Files\Common Files\Microsoft Shared\Web Server Extensions\40\Servsupp.`

When the copy is complete, the server must be rebooted.

Components

The components and administrative tools covered in this section are installed on the server by default during the initial installation. When installing the Server Extensions, the files are installed to the locations indicated here. However, keep in mind that here the C: drive is used for all paths because it is the most common drive letter for program files; this drive letter may differ on your server.

The FrontPage Server Extensions' Dynamic Link Libraries (DLL) and executable files are installed in the following:

`C:\Program Files\Common Files\Microsoft Shared\Web Server Extensions\40\Bin`

`C:\Program Files\Common Files\Microsoft Shared\Web Server Extensions\40\Servsupp.`

The ISAPI and CGI components are copied to the following:

`C:\Program Files\Common Files\Microsoft Shared\Web Server Extensions\40\Isapi`

`C:\Program Files\Common Files\Microsoft Shared\Web Server Extensions\40\_vti_bin.`

FrontPage 2000 includes three administrative tools. One of these, the graphical tool, is a snap-in to the Microsoft Management Console, `Fpmmc.dll`, which is installed to the following directory:

`C:\Program Files\Common Files\Microsoft Shared\Web Server Extensions\40\_vti_bin.`

The Server Extensions also include two command-line administrative utilities, `Fpsrvadm.exe` and `Fpremadm.exe`. Though `Fpsrvadm.exe` is used to administrate the Server Extensions, it is important to realize that it is a different utility than `Fpsrvwin.exe` and is not used to administrate the FrontPage 2000 Server Extensions in the same way that `Fpsrvwin.exe` was used in Windows NT. These two utilities are installed in the following location:

`C:\Program Files\Common Files\Microsoft Shared\Web Server Extensions\40\bin.`

See Chapter 1, "Installing and Managing IIS," for more information on the Microsoft Management Console and its snap-ins.

Administrators who prefer the HTML Administration forms can find them in the following directories:

`C:\Program Files\Common Files\Microsoft Shared\Web Server Extensions\40\Admisapi`

`C:\Program Files\Common Files\Microsoft Shared\Web Server Extensions\40\Admcgi.`

HTML Administration forms are used to remotely administer the FrontPage Server Extensions from a Web browser.

The Microsoft FrontPage 2000 Server Extensions Resource Kit (SERK), which provides complete Server Extensions documentation and is an invaluable resource for administrating the Server Extensions, is an HTML document installed in the following directory:

```
C:\Program Files\Common Files\Microsoft Shared\Web Server
Extensions\40\Serk\nnnn\default.htm
```

The \nnnn folder has a numerical name based on the language in which you installed the FrontPage Server Extensions. For example, in a U.S. English installation, the path is as follows:

```
C:\Program Files\Common Files\Microsoft Shared\Web Server
Extensions\40\Serk\1033\default.htm.
```

When a virtual server is extended by adding the FrontPage Server Extensions, additional directories are added to the home directory, or subweb. Some of the directories are created by default, while other directories will be added only when FrontPage components require them. The default directories are listed in Table 8.1.

Installing the Server Extensions to a virtual server also creates two files in the home directory of the Web site, vti_inf.html and postinfo.html. These files and directories are listed so that you will become familiar with them and their functions. More than once, I've seen a Web designer delete these "cluttering" directories and then call immediately to find out why his FrontPage Web site quit functioning correctly.

After the Server Extensions have been installed to the Web server, the individual virtual servers and subwebs, if they exist, need to be configured to make use of the Server Extensions.

Table 8.1 **FrontPage Directories**

Directory	Purpose
images	This directory stores image files.
private	This directory contains files not viewable by site visitors.
vti_cnf	For each HTML page and graphics file there is a configuration file of the same name containing name-value pairs. It identifies information, such as the last author to edit a page.
vti_log	When logging is enabled, an Author.log file is created to track the time, remote host, author's username, Web name, operation performed, and the per-operation data.
vti_pvt	This directory contains settings of the To Do list.
vti_script	This directory queries files created by the FrontPage Search component when using the Indexing Service on IIS.
vti_txt	This directory contains text indexes for the WAIS search engine.
Images	This directory stores image files.

Configuring FrontPage 2000 Extensions

Now that the installation of the Server Extensions to the Web server is complete, you need to configure the Server Extensions for each virtual server that will use the FrontPage Server Extensions. The tool of choice for most administrators is the IIS snap-in (to the MMC). You can use it to extend virtual servers, create subwebs, upgrade the Server Extensions, convert folders into subwebs (and vice versa), recalculate hyperlinks in a Web site, and much more.

Extending Virtual Servers

The FrontPage Server Extensions are installed to each virtual server after the virtual server is created in Internet Information Services. For more information on virtual servers and how to create them, refer back to Chapter 5, "Customizing WWW Sites."

Extending a virtual server by installing the Server Extensions makes the virtual server a root Web in FrontPage. A root Web is the top-most Web application in a virtual server. A virtual server can contain only one Root Web, although you can create numerous subwebs under the Root Web. To install the Server Extensions to a virtual server, simply select the virtual server and right-click on it to get the Properties menu. Select **All Tasks**, then **Configure Server Extensions**. This brings up the Server Extensions wizard, which walks you through the rest of the installation. This wizard enables you to perform the following tasks:

- Create groups and add administrators, authors, and browse access (see the section "Security Issues with FrontPage" later in this chapter for more detailed information)
- Select the Windows 2000 group or user account that will be used for administration
- Configure email options

Permissions for authoring can be set during the installation or can be added after the fact by using the IIS snap-in (to the MMC).

So far, this section has discussed a new installation of the FrontPage 2000 Server Extensions. If you already have a previous version of the FrontPage Server Extensions on your Web server, the same process will upgrade the Server Extensions. Keep in mind, though, that the existing virtual servers that are running previous versions of the Server Extensions will not automatically be upgraded. Only the default Web will be upgraded. You must extend each virtual server to upgrade the Server Extensions to FrontPage 2000.

FrontPage Server Extensions in IIS 4

In Internet Information Server 4, the FrontPage Server extensions could be installed with the click of a mouse. The Home Directory tab of a Web site included a check box labeled "FrontPage Web," which was meant to install the Server Extensions when the box was checked. Notice that this check box has been eliminated in Internet Information Services 5.

Creating and Extending Subwebs

A *subweb* is a logical division of the content of an entire Web site. A subweb can be used to break Web content into logical subdivisions to improve performance, apply a different theme or look than the root web or other subwebs, and manage hyperlinks easily.

You can create a subweb on a Root Web, on another subweb, or on a folder below the Root Web or another subweb. When you create a subweb, you can extend it with the Server Extensions at the same time. A folder is automatically created for the sub-web. Separate administering, authoring, and browsing permissions can be set for each subweb.

To create a subweb, right-click the Web (or folder) in the console tree in which you want to create a subweb. Click **New** on the shortcut menu, and then click **Server Extensions Web**. Now follow the steps in the New Subweb Wizard.

You will be prompted for the directory of the subweb, a title, and whether to keep the same administrator account/group or use a different account/group.

Administering FrontPage 2000 Server Extensions

FrontPage offers the following options for administering the Server Extensions:

- **Server Extensions snap-in (to the MMC).** The Server Extensions snap-in is by far the easiest way to administer the Server Extensions. You don't have to memorize any command-line parameters, and the only operations that cannot be performed are command-line scripting and remote management. The Server Extensions snap-in enables you to have all your administration tools under one roof.

- **HTML Administration Forms.** Another way to administer the Server Extensions remotely is with the HTML Administration Forms. When activated, these forms can be used to install and administer the server extensions over the Internet. By default, the forms are installed during the initial setup but are not active.

- **Fpsrvadm utility.** The Fpsrvadm utility can be run from a command line or used in batch files. All available configuration operations are available with the Fpsrvadm utility; however, this utility can be run only from the server on which the FrontPage Server Extensions are installed.

Securing and Activating the HTML Administration Forms

Activating the HTML Administration Forms basically requires creating and securing a virtual server or virtual directory pointing to the FrontPage Administration Forms located in C:\Program Files\Common Files\Microsoft Shared\Web Server Extensions\40\Admisapi\. Use of the HTML Administration Forms brings up some security concerns; however, these concerns are no different than those regarding the Internet in general. Follow good security guidelines, including requiring SSL, configuring NTFS permissions, and requiring account authentication. For details on all security options for Windows 2000 and Internet Information Services, review Chapter 3, "Integrating IIS with Windows 2000 Security," and Chapter 4, "IIS Security."

- **Fpremadm utility.** For remote administration from any Windows-based computer, you can use the `Fpremadm` utility. This utility is modeled after the `Fpsrvadm` utility, offers the same operations and commands, and can be used from the command line or a batch file on a remote computer. To use `Fpremadm`, you must first install the HTML Administration Forms on the server running the FrontPage Server Extensions.

- **Windows Scripting Host (WSH).** Although the Windows Scripting Host is not a part of FrontPage, it can also be used to administer a FrontPage web. The WSH is installed with Internet Information Services 5 and can be used for tasks, such as publishing webs from a development server to a production server or refreshing keyword indices. For more information on WSH, visit `http://msdn.microsoft.com/scripting/`.

Security Issues with FrontPage

Combining Server Extension security with Internet Information Services and Windows NT or Windows 2000 security will help any administrator sleep better at night. The Server Extensions provide administrative access, authoring access, and browse access using existing accounts or groups. All access to a FrontPage Web is based on the access control lists (ACLs) for each file and folder within the extended Web.

The Server Extensions use ACLs for implementing security in Internet Information Services. These ACLs are available only to files and directories on an NTFS partition, so it is imperative that the Web sites be stored on an NTFS partition. The Server Extensions also modify ACLs of system DLLs resulting from a Server Extension DLL call. The system DLLs need the correct permissions for administrators, authors, and end users for the extended Web to function correctly. This section explains how the Server Extensions authenticate users in Internet Information Services.

When an administrator or author uses the FrontPage client for any operation that uses the Server Extensions, a POST request is sent using a Remote Procedure Call (RPC) protocol. This is layered over HTTP and HTML. The administrative requests are sent to the `Admin.dll`, while the authoring requests are sent to the `Author.dll`. When a visitor accesses the Web site from a Web browser and the Server Extensions are required to fulfill the request, the browser sends a POST request to the browse-time Server Extension program, `Shtml.dll`. An example of this would be submitting a search form or returning form results via email.

When a request requires the Server Extensions, Internet Information Services logs on, impersonates the user, and passes the request first to the `Admin.dll`, then to the `Author.dll`, and finally to the `Shtml.dll`. The Server Extensions `.dll` then validates the impersonation against the ACLs on the root of the extended Web or subweb. This check is done using Windows NT or Windows 2000 system calls. If the permissions are verified, the request is fulfilled; otherwise, a "permission denied" message is returned from Internet Information Services. This happens whether the request comes from the FrontPage client or a Web browser.

Internet Information Services supports three basic types of authentication. The process for fulfilling the Server Extensions requests depends upon the authentication method(s) specified in Internet Information Services.

- **Anonymous access.** When Allow Anonymous is selected as the authentication method, the requesting user is validated against the Windows NT or Windows 2000 account database using the anonymous account specified in Internet Information Services. If the access permissions are not allowed, a "401—Access Denied" error is returned. If the ACLs are specified to allow anonymous access, the request is accepted.

- **Basic authentication.** Basic authentication is used to authenticate users—in this case, the Server Extensions administrator or authors—if this authorization scheme is selected in Internet Information Services. Basic authentication prompts the user for a login ID and password and sends this information over HTTP in a clear text format. Using basic authentication, the user logging on needs to have the right to log on locally. If the user does not have this privilege, the login will fail.

- **Integrated Windows authentication.** Integrated Windows authentication is more secure than basic authentication. This method tries to authenticate the user by using the login and password on the local computer of the requesting user. The credentials are verified without ever sending the password over the Internet. Again, just as with the other methods, if the user is authenticated against the ACLs, then that user are granted access; otherwise, the login fails and access is denied.

Integrated Windows authentication is the most secure method of authorization and thus is my recommendation, but it requires certain client operating systems and browsers. Basic authentication is the next most secure, but it does pass the user's password in clear text across the Internet. Anonymous access simply provides no security at all. For more details on these authorization methods, refer to Chapter 4.

Connecting to a FrontPage Web

So far, this chapter has discussed the Server Extensions from the administrator's view. But experience tells me that not all administrators have any idea about how the user must now take advantage of the Server Extensions. This section gives a brief overview of the user's tasks, something you may need to do—or, most likely, explain—at some point.

Any user can browse a FrontPage Web over the Internet using a Web browser. No special configurations or plug-ins are needed. Because the FrontPage components use the Server Extensions to achieve their functionality, these components reside on and are processed by the Web server. Authors should use FrontPage to publish and modify their FrontPage Webs.

When Web Browsers are used to view FrontPage Webs, they take advantage of the browse-time support functionality of the Server Extensions. FrontPage enables authors to use active components, a.k.a. WebBots, to enhance their Web site. These components are inserted into HTML pages during the authoring process as HTML code. The following are some examples of the browse-time components:

Component	Description
Search Form	The Server Extensions create a full-text index that appears as a form. The user enters words to search for, and the form returns a set of hyperlinks to the pages that contain the words.
Email Form Handler	Users can fill out information on a form page and submit it. FrontPage formats the information and sends it to a specified email address.
Discussion Form Handler	This component enables users to participate in online discussions. The information is collected from the form, formatted, and indexed. The formatted HTML page is added to a table of contents.

HTML pages that do not contain browse-time FrontPage components do not implement the Server Extensions. Internet Information Services handles requests for these pages.

Clients using FrontPage can create a Web on their client computer and then use the Publish command in FrontPage to push the files onto the Web server. Files are copied in a batch mode, so only new or changed files are copied to the Web server.

During the publishing process, Internet Information Services supplies the required name of the home page, and FrontPage changes the start page name, if necessary. Components also are generated as needed, such as Search Forms that use the indexing service.

It is also possible to work directly on a live Web server. When doing so, the changes are saved immediately when using FrontPage, so it is not necessary to publish the Web site. Although you can skip the publishing step this way, it also provides far too much leeway in destroying the functionality of a Web site, with no way of recovering except restoring a backup. I don't recommend working on a live Web site directly.

Integration with Other Services

FrontPage allows for integration with the Indexing Service, databases and SMTP servers. Each component is easy to configure and can enhance the capabilities of the Web site. The WebBots included with FrontPage are quite comprehensive and work well in the Internet Information Services environment. I encourage clients to make full use of the FrontPage components whenever possible, unless they want to learn ASP coding and Visual Basic scripting.

This section discusses integration with both the Indexing Service and SMTP servers. Database integration with Internet Information Services is not discussed here, because it is covered in Chapter 11, "Connecting to Databases."

Indexing Service

FrontPage can use the FreeWAIS search engine included with the Server Extensions, or the Indexing Service, to make the site searchable. If the Indexing Service is installed, FrontPage will default to use the Indexing Service. However, some administrators, including myself, find the Indexing Service to be bulky and difficult to work with. It also causes functionality problems when installed on the same Web server as the Server Extensions' search engine. To tell the Server Extensions not to use the Indexing Service, set the NoIndexServer configuration variable to 1 in the Registry. See the FrontPage 2000 Server Extensions Resource Kit and the Indexing Service documentation for more information.

SMTP Agents

For the Server Extensions to send a form's contents via email, the Server Extensions need to know the name or IP address of an SMTP server. This information can be supplied when initially extending the Web site or at any time thereafter. To configure the Server Extensions to access an SMTP server, click the **Settings** button in the Options section of the Server Extensions tab for the Web site properties.

This SMTP configuration is available for each virtual server. Because it is on the Web site properties page, an SMTP server cannot be configured for a subweb or for all virtual servers on a single Web server.

9

SSL and Certificate Services

THE MOST WIDESPREAD CONCERN WITH the Internet is not the limited amount of bandwidth or the occasional objectionable content, but the imperative need for security when transferring data. The most common implementation of security on the Internet today is the use of digital certificates. Digital certificates can guarantee the identity of a client or server across an untrusted network and also can encrypt data. This chapter discusses the technology behind security as well as tools provided by Microsoft for ensuring Internet security.

This chapter covers the following topics:

- Secure Sockets Layer (SSL) and why it is fundamental to security
- Encryption and its role with both clients and servers
- A description of and recommendations for client certificate mapping
- Certificates and certificate authorities on the Internet
- A complete walk-though of the installation of Microsoft Certification Authority Server

An Overview of the Secure Sockets Layer (SSL)

Internet Information Services 5 provides a high-performance implementation of Secure Sockets Layer (SSL) 3.0 for secure communication and authentication with X.509 certificates, RSA Public Key Cipher, and a broad array of additional security features. SSL enables a client communicating with a server to negotiate security and authentication levels. When a session is initiated, SSL requires a symmetric session key and encryption algorithm to be negotiated. The symmetric key is used for encrypting and decrypting data. Authentication of the client/server might also be performed while the session is being established. When the negotiation is completed, the client and the server can transmit data to each other in a secure manner by encrypting the data.

Encrypting Communication

Encryption, or *cipher*, is the means of scrambling data to ensure that it cannot be easily read by unintended recipients. The encryption features offered in Internet Information Services 5 are similar to those in Internet Information Server 4, with two exceptions: The server certificate is now bound to individual Web sites, and a new wizard helps make configuring server certificates much easier.

Configuring SSL encryption in Internet Information Services 5 is pretty much the same as in Internet Information Server 4, with one exception: You now have the capability to use Server-Gated Cryptography (SGC) certificates and encryption. SGC is available for use on banking industry sites and allows these institutions to use 128-bit encryption in export versions of Internet Information Services.

Encrypting communication between a client and a server requires configuration of both. The client, or Web browser, can support 40-bit or 128-bit encryption, or both. The server is capable of encrypting communication only after a server certificate is installed.

128-bit and 40-bit Clients

Like Microsoft Internet Explorer 5.0, Internet browsers support two encryption levels: 40-bit encryption and 128-bit encryption. 40-bit encryption is the weaker of the two; it is the maximum encryption level available for export to countries outside Canada and the United States because the U.S. government considers stronger encryption levels a threat to national security. 128-bit encryption is supported in North American versions of Internet Information Services, Internet Explorer, and Netscape Navigator.

To determine which level of encryption is installed in Internet Explorer, click the Help menu and then click the **About Internet Explorer** option. For example, in my copy of Internet Explorer 5.0, the About box lists 128-bit as the Cipher Strength.

> **Encryption versus Authentication**
>
> Although encryption and authentication are usually discussed together, they are two distinct topics. *Authentication* is the means of validating the identity of the person or processes involved in communication. Authentication can be one-way, where either party is sure about the identity of the other, or two-way, where both parties are sure of the identity of the other. Authentication with Internet Information Services 5 is covered in detail in Chapter 3, "Integrating IIS with Windows 2000 Security," and Chapter 4, "IIS Security."

Using Server Certificates

A *server certificate* is an electronic ID for your server that enables your server to perform two vital functions for secure communications: to verify its identity to users and to encrypt information going to those users. SSL encryption requires that a server certificate be bound to or associated with your Web site. This certificate contains "keys" used in forming a secure connection between your Web site and users requesting secure information.

In Internet Information Server 4, server certificates were actually bound to the Web service, not to individual Web sites, unless a Web site had a unique IP address. In Internet Information Services 5, you can bind server certificates to any Web site you want, but only one certificate per site. Also, in Internet Information Server 4, you needed to use Key Manager to bind certificates. In Internet Information Services 5, you can use the Web Site Certificate Wizard, which makes this whole process a great deal easier. The wizard guides you through the process of requesting and installing a certificate.

Client Certificate Mapping

Client certificates are the user equivalent of server certificates. A *client certificate* is a digital ID that enables a user to verify his identity to your Web server and to allow your server to use client certificate mapping. Client certificate mapping maps a client certificate to a Windows user account and automatically authenticates and allows access to users with these certificates and the proper account.

For example, if a user named Vicky has a client certificate and clicks on a link to the company Web site's Employee Information section, her Web browser sends her certificate in the request header to the server, and the server searches for a mapping for this certificate. If the user's certificate is the correct certificate and is mapped to a valid Windows user account with permissions to the content on the site, then Vicky is automatically authenticated and the requested data appears in her browser.

Types of Certificate Mapping

Two kinds of certificate mapping exist in Internet Information Services 5: one-to-one and many-to-one. *One-to-one mapping* associates a particular certificate with a particular Windows user account. An exact copy of the client certificate must reside on the server used for authentication. If the user gets another client certificate using the exact same request, the mapping will need to be remade.

Many-to-one mapping uses only certain information in the certificate and compares it against criteria to map with user accounts. As long as a certificate is used that matches these criteria, the mapping will succeed. In this way, any number of certificates can be used to map to a single user account, thus the "many-to-one" name. Copies of the certificates do not need to reside on the server.

The difference can be clarified by using some anthropomorphisms. When a request with a certificate comes in, the server has two ways of mapping it. It can say, "I'm looking for the certificate issued to Vicky on March 3, 1999, serial number ZXV345T4689AS234, and if I don't get *that* certificate, I'm sending a "403—Forbidden" error and the deal is off." Or, the server could say, "I'm looking for *any* certificate issued by the XYZ Certificate company, issued to the ABC Corporation, between March 1, 1999, and June 1, 1999. If I get *any* certificate like that, everything is cool." The first is one-to-one mapping, and the latter is many-to-one mapping.

It is easy to see that one-to-one mapping is inherently more secure, but it requires more administrative work to set up and maintain. On the other hand, many-to-one is inherently less secure, but offers greater flexibility and requires less administrative effort.

Fortezza Cards and Certificate Mapping

Smart cards make a copy of the certificate on the card and use it for mapping. After the procedure for copying the certificate is done, the certificate can be used just like any other client certificate for mapping. Typically, one-to-one mapping is used for Fortezza cards because they were designed for higher-security situations. For more information on Fortezza cards, refer to Chapter 4.

Basic Authentication with SSL

SSL encryption can be combined with basic authentication to enhance security. SSL is most often configured to encrypt data transferred to and from the Web service—for example, to encrypt a user's credit card number when making an online purchase. When SSL is combined with basic authentication, however, the user account and password are also encrypted, making this combination of security both effective and secure.

Basic authentication with SSL security is exceptionally advantageous when used for a client with a non-Microsoft browser. Clients with non-Microsoft browsers can now be authenticated by Internet Information Services and not have their username and password transferred in clear text across theInternet.

Digital Certificates

Internet Information Services also supports X.509 digital certificates for access control. These digital certificates must be issued by a trusted certificate authority and must be maintained on the client computer. They are similar in functionality to an ID card—that is, the client presents a digital certificate when attempting to access a resource on a Web server. However, these have one more level of security than a simple ID card. When the digital certificate is generated, the user must sign it with a password. Then, each time the certificate is used, the client must again enter the password to verify that the client is the actual owner of the digital certificate.

Use of digital certificates requires an appropriate protocol, such as SSL, on both the client and the server. Most often, servers present certificates to clients that authenticate the identity of the server or domain name. However, Internet Information Services can be configured to require a client to validate its identity with a client certificate.

Selecting Your Mapping Method

Which of the two mapping methods you use depends upon several factors, but the two major ones are the security level needed and the administrative resources available. If you need air-tight security and authentication, one-to-one mapping can't be beat, as long as you have the resources to handle it. If you have limited administrative resources and a large number of clients to map, then many-to-one works nicely, as long as very tight security is not needed. Following are several scenarios and recommendations for the appropriate mapping method to choose:

- **Small network with semi-secure information; authentication not needed.** Even though the network is small, many-to-one is still the way to go because the information is only semi-secure. You can create a single certificate and share it using a floppy disk.

- **Small network with semi-secure information; authentication needed.** If you want to know who is accessing what, you can use many-to-one mapping with one of the criteria being username, and map to individual user accounts. This is more work but is still better than one-to-one because users can get replacement certificates, and mappings do not need to be redone.

- **Small network with secure information; authentication needed.** In this case, it's best to go with one-to-one mapping and map certificates to individual accounts. This means that every time a user gets a replacement certificate, a new mapping will have to be made. But we're talking a small number of users. Or, you could take advantage of the Active Directory certificate features in Windows 2000. For more information about this, see the Windows 2000 documentation.

- **Large network with semi-secure information; authentication not needed.** The solution here is the same as for a small network, but you can use a different certificate for each department or group.

- **Large network with secure information; authentication needed.** For secure information, the only mapping that makes sense is one-to-one, especially if you want to enforce data responsibility. However, you may choose to go with many-to-one for its simplicity of administration. Basically, it's your call here. If you go with one-to-one, use the Active Directory to lower administration overhead.

- **James Bond.** If you want the coolest way to secure information, then one-to-one mapping with Fortezza smart cards is your aim. You can use this method to enforce policies and to secure data like nobody's business. You just suavely slide your smart card through the reader, and you're in. However, if you have large numbers of clients or you turn over clients a lot, this can be an administrative nightmare.

Server Certificates and Certificate Authorities

To activate the SSL security features of Internet Information Services, you must obtain and install a valid *server certificate*. Server certificates are digital identifications containing information about your Web server, the organization validating the server's Web content, and the fully qualified domain name (FQDN) of your site. Functioning in the same way as conventional forms of identification, a server certificate enables users to authenticate your server, check the validity of Web content, and establish a secure connection.

A digital certificate is assigned to a host by using the FQDN. Because of this, certificates are totally free of any IP address constraints. You can change the IP address of the host without any effect on the certificate. For example, if you have a certificate for the Web site `www.company.com`, it does not matter whether that domain name is referenced to the IP address 192.168.110.123 or to the IP address 123.110.168.192, or whether the IP address of the Web site changes after the certificate is issued and installed.

The success of a server certificate as a means of identification depends on whether the user trusts the validity of information contained in the certificate. For this reason, certificates are usually issued and endorsed by a mutually trusted, third-party organization, called a *Certificate Authority (CA)*. The CA's primary responsibility is confirming the identity of the organization registering a certificate. This ensures the validity of the identification information contained in the certificate.

To do this, a CA must have a *CA certificate*. The CA certificate identifies the CA that issued a server certificate, thus validating the server certificate. Of course, in this hierarchy, as in all hierarchies, there is a top. So, who validates the CA's certificate? At the very top, a CA must sign its own certificate because, by definition, there is no higher CA in the hierarchy. A self-signed CA is called a *root certificate*. Root certificates are text files with a `.crt` extension.

Alternatively, an organization can issue its own server certificates without a CA to sign them. For example, in the case of a large corporate intranet handling employee payroll and benefits information, the corporation could maintain a certificate server and assume responsibility for validating the identity of registrants and issuing server certificates.

Authentication Servers

To authenticate a server with a certificate issued by a particular CA, a client needs to verify that the issuing CA is listed in its Web browser's list of trusted CAs. The most common CA root certificates are already installed in most Web browsers.

To view the CAs that are trusted by Microsoft Internet Explorer 5, perform these steps:

1. Open Microsoft Internet Explorer 5.
2. From the Tools menu, click **Internet Options**.

3. Click the **Content** tab.

4. Click the **Authorities** button in the Certificates box.

The three tabs on the Certificate Manager dialog box contain lists of all certificates known to this copy of Internet Explorer.

Each certificate contains information about the subject and issuer of the certificate, its effective or beginning date, its expiration date, and the encoded fingerprint that identifies the certificate to other clients and servers.

To review information contained in a digital certificate, select a certificate and then click the **View Certificate** button.

To add a new CA to the list of trusted authorities for your Web server, you must explicitly add the CA's certificate, called a *root* certificate, to your Web server. You can use Microsoft Internet Explorer version 4.0 or later and a command-line utility called `Iisca.exe` to add new root certificates to your server.

Certificate Wildcard Mapping

Wildcard certificates allow multiple hosts within the same domain or subdomain to use the same digital certificate. For example, with wildcard mapping, a certificate is issued to `*.domain.com`, or simply `domain.com`, but is used to support the Web sites `http://www.domain.com` and `http://www2.domain.com`. Recall that normally a certificate is issued to one specific host, such as `www.domain.com`.

The benefit of certificate wildcard mapping is that you need to purchase only one certificate for use on multiple Web sites, making this a very cost-effective and desirable method of securing a Web site. But not all third-party CAs allow you to request a certificate that can be used on multiple hosts. Such a certificate has a common name, such as `*.domain.com` or `domain.com`. Not all Web browsers or Web servers support their use.

When a Netscape client checks the host name in this certificate, it uses a shell expansion procedure to see if it matches. In the example given, any host ending in `domain.com` should work. However, Internet Explorer does not implement wildcard certificate name checking, so Internet Explorer clients will receive a warning saying that the host name does not match that given in the certificate. In some cases, wildcards actually work with Internet Explorer 4.0 and higher, but Microsoft states officially that Internet Explorer does not work with wildcards, so there is no guarantee that wildcarding will work with any Microsoft product for any period of time.

Distributing Certificates

An organization that has determined it needs to provide certificates to clients or vendors has three general options. First, it could create its own in-house CA that meets its own security and availability requirements. Second, it could outsource its CA requirements to a third party, such as VeriSign or Thawte. Third, it could establish a chained CA with a third-party CA that allows the organization to issue certificates to end users but leverage the established security of the third-party CA.

For example, a manufacturer might decide to issue certificates to its employees across offices in three states, or a consulting firm might issue certificates to its vendors to control access to the company extranet. The organization in this example may select and purchase secure key management hardware from leading vendors, such as BBN (GTE), Chrysalis, and Atalla, or select and purchase Certificate Authority software from vendors, such as Microsoft, Xcert, or Nortel Entrust. These technologies allow the organization to issue certificates containing custom information at a security level tailored for that organization.

Unfortunately, however, most browsers will not initially recognize those certificates. Every browser that will be verifying the trustworthiness of certificates issued by that internal CA will need to be modified to acknowledge the root key used by that organization when signing the certificates. That means that every copy of Microsoft Internet Explorer, Microsoft Outlook, and Netscape Communicator needs to have the root key for the organizational CA added before data signed by these certificates will be trusted. In a small, controlled environment, that is no problem. But in a heterogeneous, multiplatform scenario such as the Internet, it is impossible.

A chained certificate program allows a third-party CA to transfer all the trust associated with the third-party CA to the organizational CA. All the software that trusts digital certificates provided by the third-party CA will immediately begin to trust the certificates issued by that chained CA.

Installing and Configuring Certificate Services

Certification Authority Server is an add-on to Windows 2000 Server that is bundled on your Windows 2000 Server installation disk. It enables you to create a customizable service for issuing and managing X509 version 3 digital certificates for authentication purposes. You can create server certificates for the Internet or for corporate intranets, giving your organization complete control over its own certificate management policies.

A wizard is included to configure the installation. Be prepared, though: You'll need to provide accurate information at the time of installation. Review the information required before attempting an installation of Certificate Services.

To install the Certification Authority Server add-on using general configuration options, use the following procedure:

1. Place the Windows 2000 Server CD-ROM into your CD drive and then select **Install Add-on Components**.

2. The Windows Components Wizard will then prompt you to select or deselect the components needed for your system. Click the check box for Certificate

Services. You will be prompted immediately with a dialog box notifying you that once certificate services have been installed, the computer cannot be renamed and cannot join or be removed from a domain.

You should address some considerations before selecting YES to continue:

- Because you will not be able to change the computer name without a reinstall of the Windows 2000 once Certification Authority has been installed, be sure that you are comfortable with the current naming convention employed on your network, or implement a new naming convention before proceeding.

- Because you will not be able to join the computer to a domain or remove it from a domain once Certification Authority has been installed, you will need to be sure that you are comfortable with the current naming convention of the domain or subdomain on your network, or implement a new naming convention before proceeding.

- Verify that the computer is joined to the appropriate domain before proceeding.

3. Next, select the Certification Authority type in the Windows Components Wizard. There are four types:

- Enterprise root CA
- Enterprise subordinate CA
- Stand-alone root CA
- Stand-alone subordinate CA

The first CA on a network must be a root CA. To create an Enterprise CA, Active Directory must be enabled. A Stand-alone CA does not require Active Directory. Select **Stand-alone root CA** to implement certificate services on your intranet. See Figure 9.1.

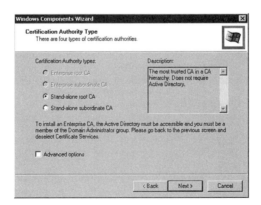

Figure 9.1 The Certificate Authority type defines not only how Certificate Services functions on you server, but also how you will need to manage it.

4. Select **CA Identifying Information** in the Windows Components Wizard. Enter the appropriate data and then continue with the install. See Figure 9.2.

5. Select the Data Storage Location in the Windows Components Wizard. I recommend that the default locations be utilized. Click **Next** to continue.

6. Click **Yes** to continue if you have Internet Information Services installed and running on your computer. Microsoft Certificate Services will inform you with a dialog box that Internet Information Services must be stopped before the install can proceed.

   The Windows Components Wizard will now configure components and copy the file on your machine. An installation progress bar is provided to monitor the installation process.

7. Click **Finish** when the Windows Component Wizard prompts you that it has completed the configuration of the components you selected.

This chapter provided a high-level discussion of certificate services in Windows 2000 because the topic is commonly misunderstood and not frequently implemented. The next chapter discusses a more common topic: SMTP and NNTP services.

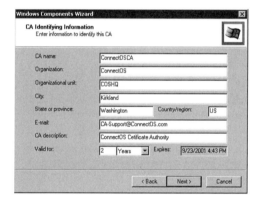

Figure 9.2   Before attempting to install Certificate Services, be sure you have all information required.

10

IIS SMTP Service
and NNTP Service

IN INTERNET INFORMATION SERVICE, MAIL DELIVERY, a very common component of Internet sites, is implemented through the use of Simple Mail Transfer Protocol (SMTP). Within the Internet Information Services snap-in (to the Microsoft Management Console), you have the ability to configure your hardware for sending and receiving messages over the Internet as well as customizing the service to meet your individual security and delivery requirements. The Microsoft SMTP service is designed with scalability, reliability, and performance as priorities, and it can support thousands of users on a single server.

The Microsoft SMTP service is installed by default during the installation of Internet Information Services. The Microsoft Management Console (MMC) is the administrative interface used to configure the SMTP service. SMTP also interfaces with other familiar administrative tools, such as Simple Network Management Protocol (SNMP), Performance Monitor, and Windows 2000 event logs. With these tools, any administrator can track messages and transactions, and collect statistics on usage and monitor performance.

This chapter covers the following topics:

- An overview of the SMTP architecture, including the process and services
- A survey of SendMail components available for use with Internet Information Services 5, locations of additional components, and coding samples
- A brief synopsis of SMTP and NNTP deployment options

- A comprehensive review of the SMTP property sheets in Internet Information Services 5
- A general discussion of NNTP and how it works

How SMTP Works

The SMTP protocol is used to transport and deliver messages. For local delivery, the messages are transferred between remote mail servers and the Drop directory on the Internet Information Services server. For remote delivery, the message is queued and then sent on to the remote server. The diagram in Figure 10.1 illustrates the process:

The SMTP service breaks down into two different components, or nodes. These nodes are listed on the left pane in the IIS snap-in underneath the SMTP virtual

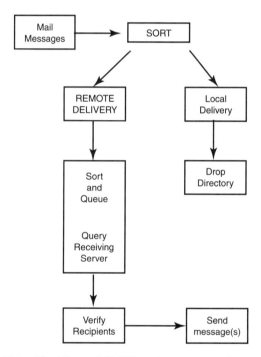

Figure 10.1   The Microsoft SMTP services process and sort messages based on a local versus remote delivery address.

RFC Compliance

The Microsoft implementation of Simple Mail Transfer Protocol (SMTP) is compliant with Request for Comments (RFCs) 821 and 822. The Microsoft implementation of Network News Transport Protocol (NNTP) is compliant with RFC 850 and RFC 977.

server. The following list gives a brief description of the services and function of each node:

- **Domains node.** Provides access to the Properties dialog box for each local, remote, or alias domain. Right-clicking the Domains node enables you to create domains; right-clicking an individual domain enables you to configure it.

- **Current Sessions node.** Lists users that are currently connected, the source location, and the length of time for each connected session.

Five default directories are created by setup when installing the SMTP service:

- **`Mailroot`.** This is the main directory. This directory must be installed on the same directory as the SMTP service and is directly below the `InetPub` directory.

- **`Badmail`.** This directory stores bad messages that can't be returned to the sender.

- **`Drop`.** The `Drop` directory receives all incoming messages. If you create multiple SMTP virtual servers on one Internet Information Services server, I recommend that each domain have its own `Drop` directory.

- **`Pickup`.** This directory is for outgoing messages.

- **`Queue`.** Messages waiting to be delivered are dropped into the `Queue` directory. If a connection can't be established with the receiving server, the message waits in the queue directory until the next retry.

If you are using the FAT file system, all the directories must remain on the same drive as the `Mailroot` directory and the SMTP service. When the partitions are NTFS, you can locate the `Badmail` and `Drop` directories on any other partition.

SendMail Components

SendMail components are more often than not used on UNIX-based systems; however, these also are available for use with Windows 2000 and Internet Information Services. The best and safest thing is to do your research before installing and configuring these components for use on your server. Once installed, these components require little to no administration.

This section discusses only two of Microsoft's SendMail components: Collaboration Data Objects and the component included with FrontPage 2000. There are certainly other options, which cannot all be listed here, but you may want to compare AspMail at `www.serverobjects.com` and other options from The ASP Resource Index at `Aspin.com`.

Collaboration Data Object (CDO)

Collaboration Data Objects (CDO) for Microsoft Windows 2000, formerly referred to as CDO 2.0, is a COM library designed to send mail through SMTP, NNTP, or

Microsoft Exchange. If you install the Microsoft SMTP server, you can send mail from an Active Server Page using CDO. Because CDO comes with the Microsoft Option Pack for Windows NT 4 and comes with Windows 2000, CDO is free.

Only a few lines of code are required to send email from an Active Server Page using CDO, as follows:

```
Set objMail = Server.CreateObject("CDONTS.NewMail")
objMail.Send "fromuser@domain.com","touser@domain.com","Test Mail",
"This is a test mail using CDO",0
Set objMail = nothing
```

When you create the Newmail object, you are actually creating a CDO session and logging into the SMTP server that is installed on the same system as the Web Server. To do this, you must also install Microsoft's SMTP server, which also comes with the option pack for Windows NT 4 and comes with Windows 2000. Assuming that you have a DNS server to resolve the MX and A records, the SMTP server will deliver the email.

After the email is sent, the Newmail object becomes invalid. It is good coding practice to set the Newmail object to Nothing after its use to ensure that the object's resources are released. To send another piece of email, you must recreate the Newmail object.

Because CDO is integrated with Windows 2000, it is quick and easy to set up. In addition, the configuration can easily be modified if you want to switch to a Microsoft Exchange Server in the future. On the downside, the CDO does not supply any error messages or responses, because it doesn't do any checking for performance purposes.

FrontPage 2000 Server Extensions

Clients who are using the FrontPage 2000 Server Extensions for developing their sites will likely want to use the SMTP component available within the extended site properties. When extending a virtual server to use the FrontPage 2000 extensions, you are prompted for the mail server identification, which may be an IP address, and the default addresses from which the mail message will be sent. This is the most convenient method of configuration on the server from a development standpoint. The client needs to know only the name or the IP address to which the message will be transported, and the SMTP service takes care of the rest.

One of the limitations of the FrontPage 2000 SendMail component is that it can be configured only for a virtual server, not for a specific Web site. For more information on the FrontPage 2000 Server Extensions, refer to Chapter 8, "Microsoft

Error Handling in the Newmail Object

No SMTP error checking occurs in the Newmail object. The object submits the email to the SMTP server, where it is either sent or rejected. The script running the object does not get an error code from the object because the process takes place on the SMTP server. Any delivery errors in the email will be forwarded from the SMTP server to the From (that is, the sender's) email address.

FrontPage Server Extensions;" for a more detailed discussion of them, I recommend the *Official Microsoft FrontPage 2000 Book* from Microsoft Press.

Other Mail Solutions

SMTP services are part of the Internet Information Services portion of Windows 2000, which makes them easy to set up. The setup is all wizard-based, as with most other of the Internet Information Services components. But this is not the only option.

Another solution is Microsoft Exchange, which is a great option for internal mail. In addition, this program is very fast and easy to connect to the Internet. On the other hand, Microsoft Exchange does not allow for multiple domains and is not the most cost-efficient option available.

Many third-party options for using SMTP configured via the server also exist. Some key features to look for include scalability, security, ease of administration, and compatibility with clients and your server software. One product with these features that is used at our company is Post.Office, by Software.com.

The Post.Office interface is browser-based and is very easy to navigate. As the post-master, you are given the option of restricting user privileges, such as changing their passwords, setting their auto-responders, and viewing their mailbox directory information. Various licensing options and packages are available to suit the needs of any company. For more detailed information about this software, check out www.software.com.

SMTP Site Properties

The SMTP site property sheet is used to set connection parameters for identification, connections, and logging configuration for a site from which you need to send mail with the Microsoft SMTP service. The parameters include identifying the correct port to be used, designating the number of connections that can be opened simultaneously, limiting the length of time before a connection remains open, and enabling or disabling logging for each site.

General Properties

The General tab of the SMTP site property sheet is fairly self-explanatory for configuration. Through this site, you designate the SMTP site identification via a description and an IP address.

To configure incoming and outgoing connections, you must identify the TCP/IP port used for the connections, as well as designate connection timeouts and connection limitations on a per-domain basis. All these options have a set default. You'll need to specify an IP address, unless you have only one SMTP virtual server, but I recommend that you use the default port 25. In addition to providing identification and connection information, this interface allows you to enable logging for the SMTP site and to choose your log file format. For more information on log file formats, see Chapter 12, "Managing Log Files." From this tab, you can also choose properties that specifically define timelines for creating new logs and defining file directories for the logs.

Access

The Access tab enables you to configure the following information:

- **Access control.** Configure authentication methods for accessing the SMTP virtual server. For information on authentication methods, look back at Chapter 4, "IIS Security."

- **Secure communication.** Configure the use of certificates for Secure Sockets Layer (SSL) communication. For information on SSL and certificates, see Chapter 9, "SSL and Certificate Services."

- **Connection control.** Grant or deny access to this virtual server based on IP address and domain name restrictions. For information on configuring this, review Chapter 4.

- **Relay restrictions.** This option enables you to control domains that send email through this SMTP virtual server. For example, if I configure an SMTP virtual server for kadam.com, I don't want a user making up a sender address and using my SMTP server to originate his email. Most users who do this do not have the best intentions, so it is important to restrict this type of use.

Messages

Within this property sheet, you can set limits for messages, including the size and the number of recipients that can receive the message. For example, if a message is sent that exceeds the limits that are set, the message will become undeliverable and will be returned to the sender along with a non-delivery-report (NDR). If the NDR proves to be undeliverable as well, the message is sent to the Badmail directory. The Badmail directory, as well as the storage for NDRs and bad mail, is defined on this property sheet.

Other properties defined within this sheet include limiting the number of outbound messages per connection and the number of recipients per message. In addition, receiving parties of an NDR generated by Microsoft SMTP Service can be configured on this sheet.

Delivery

The configuration of your delivery options is divided into outbound and local delivery. The default for these options is fine, unless you have a specific requirement. Some of the options include retry intervals, delay notifications, and expiration timeouts.

Advanced options include defining the maximum hop count, the fully qualified domain name (the address used in the message exchanger [MX] record in your DNS server), and the smart host or server that all outgoing messages are routed through.

LDAP Routing

Lightweight Directory Access Protocol (LDAP) routing enables you to specify a directory services server with which the SMTP virtual server can communicate by using LDAP. An LDAP server stores information about mail clients and can resolve senders and recipients. LDAP routing is an excellent way to integrate Windows 2000 Active Directory users into mailing lists. It can also be used to integrate user information from both the site server membership directory and Microsoft Exchange.

Security

The Security tab is similar to the Operators tab in the WWW properties sheet. Use this tab to give specific user accounts permission as operators for this SMTP virtual server. However, as with WWW sites, there is little need to add operators, so you should not have to configure this tab.

NNTP Service

The Network News Transport Protocol (NNTP) service that is part of Internet Information Services is a fully functional service for providing users a forum for posting and reading information of interest. Newsgroups can be restricted to within your organization or can be publicly available on the Internet. The Microsoft NNTP format is compatible with other NNTP clients and servers, offering scalability and support for various content formats, including these:

- Multipurpose Internet Mail Extension (MIME)
- Hypertext Markup Language (HTML)
- Graphics Interchange Format (GIF)
- Joint Photographic Experts Group (JPEG)

Allowing all these different formats enables users to include pictures and Web links within articles that they post.

Restricting Spam

To limit the proliferation of unsolicited commercial mail (UCE), or *spam* (special offers, commentaries, or any messages a sender wants to convey to as many recipients as possible), the SMTP service, by default, doesn't allow mail to be relayed through it to an external email address. To allow mail to be relayed from specific IP addresses or domain names, you must change the settings in the Relay Restrictions section of the Access tab. Changing these settings makes your site a prime target for UCE.

Configuring SMTP Domains

The SMTP service is installed along with and has identical system requirements to Internet Information Services. The setup is wizard-based and asks for all the typical information, such as the domain name, a description, and an IP address.

Process Overview

The NNTP service process will vary depending on whether the newsgroups are moderated or not moderated. In a nonmoderated environment, the user submits an article, and that article is posted to the directory and is available to other newsgroup users. If the newsgroup is moderated, after the user submits the article, the moderator can approve or reject the submission. If approved, the article is posted to the newsgroup. If rejected, the article is discarded and a rejection notice is sent to the user who submitted the article.

Setting up moderated newsgroups requires either an SMTP mail server to send articles to a moderator's directory, or a directory that the moderators can access and retrieve the files.

Directories

Each newsgroup has its own directory, and the articles are stored within the directory as files. The main directory is located at X:\Inetpub\nntproot, where X:\ is the drive on which Internet Information Services was installed. This directory can be changed to another physical drive or even another computer. This can be done by configuring virtual directories.

The newsgroup directories exist below the nntproot directory. The directories are automatically created when you create a new nntp newsgroup, and the directories are named the same as the newsgroup itself. An example of this would be a newsgroup named business.news, which would be located in the directory X:\InetPub\nntproot\business\news.

The articles have the default extension of .nws. The NNTP service also creates a file that will list the subject of each stored article, and gives these files an .xix extension. Each one of these files lists 128 articles within the newsgroup. If more articles exist, another file with the .xix extension will be created for that newsgroup.

Internal data structure files are automatically created when the NNTP service is installed. These files are located off the InetPub root, in a directory named Nntpfile. These files have .hsh, .hdr, .lst, and .txt extensions, and they should not be modified or deleted. Any changes to these files could render the NNTP service useless.

Services

The NNTP service is not installed as a component of Internet Information Services by default. When installing Internet Information Services, you must go into the Custom option to add the service. The requirements for the NNTP service are the same as those for Internet Information Services. As a system administrator, you have the ability to log on to the server and start, stop, or pause the service as needed. This can be done through the MMC.

NNTP is a client/server protocol, with the service being the server side, and clients using a mail and news client to receive the articles. TCP/IP is used for client connections to the server. The default port is 119 or, for SSL connections, port 563. Clients can post articles using their news client. They must establish a connection to the server and be authenticated by the NNTP service. If authentication is verified, the article is posted to the specified newsgroup(s).

As with most property sheets for various service components of Internet Information services, the property sheets associated with the NNTP service are self-explanatory. Using the various tabs, you can configure directory locations, determine whether the newsgroup is moderated, establish security settings, and determine when articles will expire, in addition to many other properties. Most of the configuration options on these tabs have been discussed in this chapter or are covered in other sections of this book. Additional information is accessible via the Help button on the property sheet.

11

Connecting to Databases

INTERNET INFORMATION SERVER HAS ALWAYS provided a mechanism for connecting to a database. In the beginning, database connectivity was provided through an Internet Database Connector (IDC). IDC matured as Internet Information Server matured; however, it never really provided a simple way to access data. With IDC, a Web developer needed to write either a Common Gateway Interface (CGI) program or an Internet Server Application Programming Interface (ISAPI) application to efficiently work with the database. I've generally found ISAPI to be too complex for most Web developers and CGI to require too many system resources.

With Internet Information Server 3 came Active Server Pages (ASP). ASPs enable Web developers to embed scripts in their Web pages to easily access databases. Many Web developers today use ASPs for a variety of tasks, including database access, because they are simple to learn, easy to write, and can provide a wide range of functionality. For more information on ASPs, see Chapter 7, "Running Web Applications."

This chapter describes the components that make up the Microsoft Universal Data Access (UDA) solution. As the administrator of an Internet Information Services server, you will undoubtedly receive requests from Webmasters who want to store data to, or retrieve data from, a database. Therefore, this chapter covers the various methods used to connect to a database and select the correct database access method.

This chapter covers the following topics:

- An architectural overview of Open Database Connectivity, highlighting its components

- Three methods of connecting to a database, including configuring a system data source name, configuring a file data source name, and creating a data source name by using Active Server Pages code

- The pros and cons to using Microsoft SQL Server databases and Microsoft Access databases

- Version checking and its value to database connectivity

- A preventative measure for securing Open Database Connectivity information

Microsoft Data Access Components

Most Internet Information Services Web developers will store data in either a Microsoft SQL Server database or a Microsoft Access database. To provide access to this data, Microsoft offers a set of components appropriately called Microsoft Data Access Components (MDAC). MDAC provides a set of relatively easy-to-use, high-performance components that grant a Web developer access to all types of data on a network. If Web developers are creating client/server and network-based data-driven solutions, they will most likely use these components to easily integrate information from a variety of sources, both relational and nonrelational.

MDAC is comprised of ActiveX Data Objects (ADO), Object Linking and Embedding Database (OLE DB), and Open Database Connectivity (ODBC). For more details on MDAC and Microsoft's Universal Data Access, connect to `http://www.microsoft.com/data/`.

ADO Model

The ADO model provides Web developers with a flexible method of accessing content stored in a database. In the ADO model, a Web developer calls an ADO object from script code within Active Server Pages (ASP) code both to query a database for information and to submit data to a database. The ADO object then calls an ADO provider, such as an ODBC driver talking to a Microsoft Access database, an SQL Server ODBC/OLE-DB driver talking to a SQL Server database, or an OLE-DB driver talking to Microsoft Index Server. Figure 11.1 shows the logical layers between the ASP code and the database.

As you can see, the same ASP code can talk to any ADO provider as long as an ODBC interface exists, and there are a lot of them, ranging from Microsoft's SQL Server to IBM's DB2—there's even one for a flat text file.

If a Web developer asks you, as the Web server administrator, what he will need to access a database, you should recommend using the ADO interface and writing ASP code to communicate with the database. The combination of the ADO interface and ASP code will provide the most flexibility in database choices and also will give you a simple way of supporting the Web developer, no matter how complicated the database.

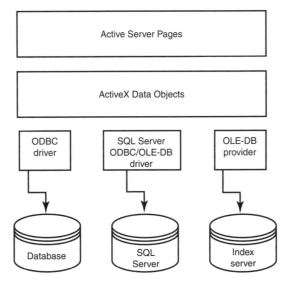

Figure 11.1   The ADO model allows for access to multiple databases by supporting multiple database drivers.

ActiveX Data Objects Overview

Microsoft ActiveX Data Objects (ADO) are designed to interface with relational databases through Open Database Connectivity (ODBC). As long as the company creating the database type provides an ODBC driver for its database model, you can access the database through ASP code or any Microsoft product. Currently ODBC drivers exist for a wide array of database types, including Microsoft SQL Server, Microsoft Access, IBM DB2, and Oracle. ADO is built on top of OLE DB, which is discussed in the next section. More information on ADO can be found at this site: http://www.microsoft.com/data/ado/.

OLE DB

OLE DB is a set of interfaces for data access and Microsoft's component database architecture that provides universal data integration over an enterprise network, regardless of the data type. Microsoft's ODBC data access interface continues to provide a unified way to access relational data as part of the OLE DB specification. Over time, OLE DB is expected to lead new database products that are assembled from best-in-class components rather than from the monolithic products available today.

OLE DB provides a flexible and efficient database architecture that offers applications, compilers, and other database components efficient access to Microsoft and third-party data stores. OLE DB is the fundamental Component Object Model (COM) building block for storing and retrieving records, and it unifies Microsoft's strategy for database connectivity. COM will be used throughout Microsoft's line of applications and data stores.

OLE DB defines interfaces for accessing and manipulating all types of data. These interfaces will be used not just by data-consuming applications, but also by database providers. By splitting databases apart, the resulting components can be used in an efficient manner. For example, components called *service providers* can be invoked to expose more sophisticated data manipulation and navigation interfaces on behalf of simple *data providers*. For more information on OLE DB, see `http://www.microsoft.com/data/olddb/`.

Open Database Connectivity (ODBC)

ODBC is an Application Programming Interface (API) that uses Structured Query Language (SQL) as its database access language. Database applications call functions in the ODBC interface, which are implemented in database-specific modules called drivers. The use of drivers isolates applications from database-specific calls in the same way that printer drivers isolate word processing programs from printer-specific commands. Because drivers are loaded at run time, a user only has to add a new driver to access a new database type; it is not necessary to recompile or re-link the application to the new database even if the database type changes. For more information on ODBC, see `http://www.microsoft.com/data/odbc/`.

How to Make the Connection

Whatever type of database the Web developer is going to connect to, he will need to know where the database is physically located. In most cases, that may mean creating a Data Source Name (DSN). In my experience, most database access requires that a System DSN be configured on the Internet Information Services server. But because you may run across a couple other common types of connection requests, this section elaborates on them.

Before you can connect to a database, you will need to have the following information available:

- **Server.** The name of the server containing the database. When connecting to an Access database, the database will probably reside on the same server as Internet Information Services. When connecting to an SQL Server database, the database should reside on a server other then the Web server because of the resources required to run both Internet Information Services and SQL Server. It is possible to run both on the same server and is very cost-effective, but you should not attempt this unless you expect very few connections to both the Web server and the database. In the following examples, COSSQL is used as the server name.

- **Database.** The name of the database. The following examples refer to the PUBS database that is installed as part of Microsoft SQL Server.

- **Driver.** The name defining the type of database driver.
- **User ID and password.** The logon name presented to the database for access when connecting to the database, and the password required for that username.

Three common ways exist by which to connect to a database:

- System DSN
- File DSN
- "On-the-fly" DSN

As the Web server administrator, you will most likely need to create a System DSN for each database being accessed from a Web site, create a database device if accessing Microsoft SQL Server, and create the database. The System DSN resides on the Internet Information Services server. Its role is to locate the database, whether it be on a local or remote server.

System DSN

A System DSN is designed to be used by any service or process running on that server. The most common way to create a DSN is through the ODBC Data Source Administrator. The following example creates a System DSN to an SQL Server database called PUBS. The PUBS database is installed as a sample database with both SQL Server 6.5 and SQL Server 7.0.

1. Click **Start**, **Programs**, **Administrative Tools**, and then click **Data Sources (ODBC)**.
2. Click the **System DSN** tab, and then click **Add**. You will be prompted with the Create New Data Source dialog box. See Figure 11.2.
3. Select the data source driver, and then click **Finish**. You will be prompted with a dialog box to create a data source for the specific driver you chose in the Create New Data Source dialog box.

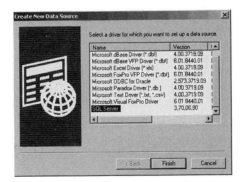

Figure 11.2 Select the data source driver from the Create New Data Source dialog box.

4. Type in a name and description for the data source, followed by the server on which the database exists (see Figure 11.3). In this example, you are creating a DSN that points to the PUBS database on the COSSQL server. Then, click **Next**.

5. Next, specify the login account that will be used to access the database on the server. If you expect to host more than one customer's database on one SQL Server, I recommend that you select the **With SQL Server authentication using a login ID and password entered by the user** radio button. I also recommend that you leave the "Connect to SQL Server to obtain default settings for the additional configuration options" check box selected. Fill in the Login ID and Password fields with a valid SQL Server account. Because of the potential security concerns, do not use the SQL Server system administrator (sa) account to access your customers' databases. See Figure 11.4.

6. Click the **Client Configuration** button. The Add Network Library Configuration dialog box will appear. Verify that the TCP/IP radio button is selected. Click **OK** and then click **Next**.

7. Verify that the database you will connect to is listed on the Create New Data Source to SQL Server dialog box. If the correct database is not selected, then select the "Change Default database to:" check box, and enter the correct database name. Click **Next** to continue.

8. Click **Finish** to accept the default selections in the next dialog box and view the summary of the connections.

9. Select the **Test** button in the ODBC Microsoft SQL Server Setup dialog box. Always test the data source; don't assume anything. See Figure 11.5.

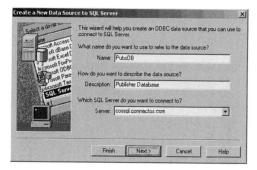

Figure 11.3   The data source name and description are only for administrative information, but the server name must be valid.

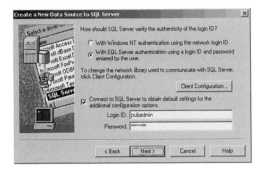

Figure 11.4 Authentication to an SQL Server is the most important security decision you will make when connecting to an SQL database.

Figure 11.5 Verify all configured information before testing the new data source.

Typical data source failures include these:

- The SQL username does not exist, the password is not correct, or the account does not have access to the database.
- The SQL Server name is incorrect or cannot be found, or the database name does not exist.
- This is an Internet environment, and TCP/IP is not selected in the client configuration dialog box.

If everything was configured correctly, clicking the test data source button will result in a dialog box stating, "Test completed successfully!"

10. Click **OK** to return to the ODBC Data Source Administrator dialog box with the System DSN tab selected. Your new data source will be listed.

File DSN

A File DSN is similar to a System DSN, except that a File DSN is generally user-specific. File DSNs are most often used by developers working locally on a development system with a developer version of SQL Server installed on the same server. File DSNs were designed to be stored on a server and used only by applications on that server. The configuration of a File DSN is the same as the configuration of a System DSN. However, as the administrator of an Internet Information Services server, you will probably never need to configure a File DSN.

DSN-less Connection

When creating a System DSN, you created the DSN from the ODBC Data Source Administrator. Another option to using this utility is to create a DSN-less connection, or an "on-the-fly" DSN. With a DSN-less connection, the information required to access the database is written into the ASP code. A DSN-less connection not only saves the developer the trouble of requesting that the administrator create a DSN, but it also opens up powerful possibilities for dynamic applications.

When a DSN-less connection is created, it still does not connect directly to the database. It instead connects to the ODBC driver and passes it the information needed to attach to the database. In this case, the ODBC driver becomes the data provider for the database application.

To programmatically create a DSN-less connection, you only need to execute the following lines of ASP code within the Web page that writes to or reads from the database:

```
DBConn.Open "DRIVER={Microsoft Access Driver (*.mdb)}; " &
    "DBQ= c:\Inetpub\iissamples\sdk\asp\database\Authors.mdb"
```

In this example, a database connection is opened to a Microsoft Access database stored in the `authors.mdb` file. After the application has finished using this DSN-less connection, the connection must be closed.

A DSN-less connection is more convenient than a System DSN and is quicker to create. A DSN-less connection is most likely created to connect to a local database, such as Microsoft Access database stored in an `.mdb` file. One reason a Web developer might choose a DSN-less connection is because he does not have to request or supply information to the Web server administrator, so the Web administrator never will know that a database is being utilized on a Web site.

However, with all databases (including both remote SQL databases as well as local Access databases), a System DSN is more efficient. Also, when using an authoring environment, such as Microsoft Visual Interdev, its powerful database tools function and perform better by using a System DSN.

Microsoft SQL Server versus Access

The big debate in Web-based database connectivity is when to use a Microsoft SQL Server database versus a Microsoft Access database. In most cases, the Web developer will already know which one he wants to use. But if the Web developer is unsure, ask some of the following questions:

- Are you already familiar with SQL Server and its query tools? If not, then creating SQL tables by submitting queries to the server or bulk-loading data into the tables may be too complex.

- How many Web users do you expect to generate database queries at any moment? If the answer is more than about 25, then the Web application will probably require a SQL Server database.

- How do you plan to administer the database? It is very easy to use Microsoft Access to create, populate, and upload an Access database. SQL Server will require more complex tools.

SQL Server offers more complex and less user-friendly interfaces than Access offers. The Access interface makes it easy to view and edit data in the Access database file. SQL Server does provide several tools to simplify its use, such as ISQLW in SQL Server 6.5, but these tools are not nearly as user-friendly as the Access interface.

Of course, the primary reason to use SQL Server is performance. SQL Server can support a massive number of users and queries at one time—and a great deal quicker than Access ever could. SQL Server also provides powerful options for creating stored procedures, or pre-built queries. What's more, SQL Server is a true service that runs as a background task. If data integrity and exceptional performance are required, the Microsoft SQL Server is your database answer.

Version Checking

As MDAC is enhanced, you will probably need to periodically update your MDAC components. Monitor `http://www.microsoft.com/data/` for the latest MDAC version. Problems related to incorrect versioning are usually very clear. For example, when I was administering a shared server running Internet Information Server 4, one of the Web developers decided to upgrade his Access database file to Access 2000.

SQL Server Internet Licensing

If you choose to offer and manage a Microsoft SQL Server, verify that you have an adequate number of licenses to support your customer base. SQL Server ships with 10 Client Access Licenses (CALs), which means that no more than 10 Web clients can be connected to the SQL Server at the same time. Individual CALs are very expensive, so if you expect a lot of connections, look into the SQL Server Internet Connector License, which provides for an unlimited number of simultaneous connections to an SQL Server from Web clients.

So, he simply copied the new Access 2000 database file over his existing Access 97 database file. Suddenly, his database stopped working. To correct the problem, he could have copied his old database file back to the server, or I could have installed the latest ODBC interface to the Web server—which I did.

At the time of this writing, the current shipping version of MDAC is 2.1.2.4203.3. Although it's a bit complicated to check the version of MDAC under Windows NT 4, it is pleasantly simple with Windows 2000. To determine whether your Web server contains the most recent updates, click the Windows Update option on the Start menu. This is invaluable information for an Internet Information Services administrator.

Security Issues

When allowing access to a database from a Web client, keep some additional security considerations in mind. If the database, data source, or ASP code is not properly secured, Web clients may be able to access portions of the database to which they should not be authorized, or they may be able to modify or even delete crucial data.

The following list highlights three of the most common security concerns when accessing a database from a Web site:

- Do not place an Access database file, an `.mdb` file, into a directory that allows the anonymous Web user simple access to download the entire database file.

- Do not place the username and password required to access a database within the DSN on a shared server. This might allow other Web developers on the same server to call your DSN and access your database.

- With Internet Information Server 4, verify that you have installed the `::$DATA` security patch. With Internet Information Services 5, verify that you have not allowed script source permissions on the directory containing the ASP pages used to access the database. In either case, a Web client can request the source code for an ASP page and obtain the data source name, username, and password needed to access a database.

Database access from a Web page can be a very powerful tool and can enable Web developers to provide flexible, dynamic content. Now that you have reviewed all content configuration for an Internet Information Services server, you can determine how your content is accessed by looking at log files generated by Internet Information Services.

Microsoft Windows Update

I highly recommend that you take advantage of the Microsoft Windows Update option. Either schedule a time to check for new updates and components on a frequent schedule, or enable the auto notification option so that you are automatically notified of new updates as they become available. You will never again worry about the latest security patches or components for your Internet Information Services server. You can connect to the Web site directly by connecting to http://windowsupdate.microsoft.com/.

12

Managing Log Files

INTERNET INFORMATION SERVICES ENABLES YOU to log activity on each Web site. The resulting log files can then be used to analyze traffic on the server as a whole or for each individual virtual server.

This chapter covers the following topics:

- The log file formats available in Internet Information Services 5 and the benefits of each
- Utilities that will interpret log file data and generate valuable statistics and reports
- Recommendations for managing log files on servers

Understanding Log File Formats

With previous versions of Internet Information Server, each virtual server's activity was contained within a single directory. A new logging architecture was introduced with Internet Information Server 4 that improved performance and allowed for greater flexibility. Now, activity can be separated into distinct directories for each Web site configured on a server.

Although logging provides many benefits, trying to log every access for every service will certainly cause deterioration in performance. Administrators can choose which resources are logged, how often log files are generated, and which files are included in the logging process to limit this effect on performance.

In general, logging FTP or SMTP services is not necessary and creates extra activity on the server. You will usually not want to enable logging for these services unless you need to troubleshoot a specific issue.

To generate log files for a Web site, check the "Enable Logging" check box on the Web Site tab of the Web Site Properties dialog box. You must also select a log format and might want to configure additional properties. The next section discusses each of the log file formats and the benefits of that specific format.

On the General Properties tab of the Extended Logging Properties dialog box for all log file formats, you can specify that a new log file be generated hourly, daily, weekly, or monthly. Two additional options allow you to instead base new logs on the size of the log file: either "Unlimited file size" or "When the file size reaches" a configured size in megabytes (MB).

The frequency with which you need to generate reports should help determine the time period you select. From my experience with maintaining log files and generating reports, I suggest that you stick with the default selection of a daily format for most Web sites. This lets you run a report for a specific day if the site is having a special promotion or is featured on a popular site. With some reporting programs, daily statistics will also provide details about hits, accesses, and additional information on a daily basis. Many clients like to see items, such as which day of the week the site is being accessed the most. Different reporting software enables you to generate reports with different options. With the reporting tool you choose, it may not matter with which frequency log files are generated. The reporting tool may be capable of pulling information from multiple log files at once or from a portion of a larger log file.

Another consideration in selecting the logging time period is the amount of traffic to the Web site, and, thus, the rate at which the log files grow. For example, it would be impossible for Microsoft to generate weekly log files for www.microsoft.com. The log files would just be too big to store or manage.

You should consider many factors if you are going to specify a size limit for the log files: How many virtual servers are configured on the Web server? What log file format will you use? How much space is on the drive that contains the log files? In general, it is not necessary to limit the size of the log files unless you are low on available disk space. If this is the case, you should probably configure the log file directories to a different drive partition that has the capacity to store the log files.

The remainder of this section discusses the four log file formats available in Internet Information Services 5: Microsoft IIS Log File Format, NCSA Common Log File Format, ODBC Logging, and W3C Extended Log File Format.

Microsoft IIS Log File Format

The Microsoft IIS Log File Format is the original log file format created by Microsoft for Internet Information Server. The information is written as a comma-delimited, fixed ASCII text file and is not customizable like other log file formats available in Internet Information Services.

Hopefully, you will select a log file analyzer to decipher the information in the log files. Still, to choose the log file format that is best suited to a particular Web site, you should know what data is stored in the log file. The following is a sample line from a log file generated using Microsoft IIS Extended Log File Format:

```
123.456.789.1, connectos.com, 8/18/97, 13:17:37, WWW, COSWEB, 209.67.75.200, 481,
34, 52, 200, 0, GET, /press.htm
```

Each line in the log file contains the same entries. If data for a specific entry cannot be determined, that field is marked with a dash (–) in the log line. The following fields are logged in order: Client IP Address, User, Date, Time, Service, Server Name, Server IP address, Elapsed Time, Bytes Received, Bytes Sent, Service Status, Win32 Status, Name of Operation, and Target.

NCSA Common Log File Format

The NCSA format you choose will enable you to see the similarities among the other various formats. The following example shows the fields logged into an ASCII text file:

```
209.67.73.73 — COSHQ\COSTECH [13/Apr/1998:17:39:04 -0800] "GET
/scripts/iisadmin/ism.dll?http/serv, HTTP/1.0" 200 3401
```

The fields are Remote Host Name, User's Username, Date, Time & GMT Offset, Request, Service Status, and Bytes Sent.

ODBC Logging

Another option for logging is to log Web site requests to an Open Database Connectivity (ODBC) database. To log to an ODBC database, you will need to configure the Data Source Name (DSN), table, and specify the username and password to use when logging to the database.

A key difference between ODBC logging and other logging options is that with ODBC logging, one single transmission creates multiple records. Because of these multiple entries, OBCS logging requires more server resources than the other logging methods and might affect the performance of the Web server, depending on database type, location, and amount of logged entries.

The following list is an example of the fields that ODBC logs generate:

- **Clienthost.** Client IP address.
- **Username.** Client domain name.
- **Logtime.** Connection date and time.
- **Service.** Internet Information Server service.
- **Machine.** Computer name.
- **ServerIP.** Server IP address.

- **ProcessingTime.** Processing time in milliseconds.
- **BytesRecvd.** Bytes received by server.
- **BytesSent.** Bytes sent by server.
- **ServiceStatus.** Protocol reply code.
- **Win32Status.** Windows 2000 Server status or error code.
- **Operation.** Protocol command.
- **Target.** Recipient.

W3C Extended Log File Format

The W3C format is an industry-standard log file format that offers more flexibility than the other formats by enabling you to choose what fields are actually logged. Because of this feature, you can gather details about fields that are important to you and your clients, while limiting log size by omitting fields that are not needed. The logged fields are written to an ASCII text file. Figure 12.1 displays the Extended Properties tab available when logging using the W3C Extended Log File Format.

Because you have the option of individually selecting fields to be logged, a brief overview of the options is necessary. Most of the options are rather self-explanatory, but a quick review can help you understand which fields have information that may be more important for your analysis needs. The following list of options includes a brief description of each:

Figure 12.1 Only W3C Extended Log File Format enables you to select and deselect specific fields for inclusion in the log files.

Concerns with the Date Field

If you are creating a daily log file, a date stamp is placed at the top of the log file, making the Date field unnecessary. If the Date field is selected, then the date of the request will be logged on each line of the log file. By default, the Date field is not selected because it is generally unnecessary and can increase the size of your log files by almost 10%.

- **Date.** The date that the activity occurred.
- **Time.** The time that the activity occurred.
- **Client IP Address.** Identity of the user accessing the site by IP address.
- **User Name.** The name of the user.
- **Service Name.** The service that is being used—such as www, ftp, and so on—on the client machine.
- **Server Name.** The name of the server.
- **Server IP Address.** The IP address of the server.
- **Method.** This usually shows as GET, which is a request; otherwise, it shows the action.
- **URI Stem.** The path of the request, such as HTML request, cgi program, or script access.
- **URI Query.** The search string if a query is the action.
- **Protocol status.** A record of successes and failures.
- **Win32 status.** A zero indicates no errors; a number indicates the particular error.
- **Bytes sent.** The amount in bytes sent by the server.
- **Bytes received.** The amount in bytes received by the server.
- **Time taken.** The amount of time to fulfill the action.
- **Protocol Version.** The version of the protocol being used by the client.
- **User Agent.** The browser, version, and operating system of the user.
- **Cookie.** The content of the cookie sent or received, if any.
- **Referrer.** Where the user came from, such as a link from another Web site.

The following lines are a sample from a W3C extended log file, along with the header information:

```
#Software: Microsoft Internet Information Server 5.0
#Version: 1.0
#Fields: date time c-ip cs-username s-ip cs-method cs-uri-stem cs-uri-query sc-
➥ status sc-bytes cs-bytes time-taken cs-version cs(User-Agent) cs(Cookie)
➥ cs(Referrer)
1998-10-04 00:10:13 209.67.64.254 - 209.67.75.100 GET /images/bo_animated.gif -
➥ 200 16086 271 187
HTTP/1.0 Mozilla/4.05+[en]+(WinNT;+I) - http://www.connectos.com/
```

As you can see, a lot of information can be eliminated from the log, which will save valuable hard drive space on your Web server.

Generating Reports from Log Files

When a logging option is selected, you must decide how you would like to generate your log reports. Many options are available for generating reports with the different formats of log files. This section covers the various reporting technologies available, including some third-party utilities.

Site Server Express

Site Server Express can be used to analyze log files by using the Usage Import and Report Writer modules. The log files are imported into an Access database. The predefined reports provide traffic features, such as requests, visits, users, and organizations, that interact with the Web sites.

The first step in using Site Server Express is to import the log files. The following steps walk you through the configuration:

1. Start Usage Import.

2. Configure an Internet site using the Server Manager.

3. Create a data source with the appropriate log file type by right-clicking the Log Data Sources icon, and then click **New**.

4. Specify a server by right-clicking the scroll icon, and then click **New**.

5. Configure a site by right-clicking the newly created server icon, and then click **New**.

6. Open the Log file manager (from the **File** menu or from the toolbar), and type in the path to your log file or identify it using the **Browse** button.

7. Press the green **Start import** button on the toolbar to begin the import.

After the log files have been imported, use the Report Writer to generate a report. To accomplish this, do the following:

1. Start Report Writer.

2. Click the **Create an analysis report** button from the catalog option.

3. Select a report to run, such as Executive Summary.

4. Click **Finish** on the first option panel.

5. From the schematic representation of your report content, click the green **Create report document** button. The default is an HTML report, which will be opened with your browser upon completion.

Site Server Express is fairly simple to use. You can create custom reports, and you can generate reports not only in HTML format, but also in Microsoft Word or Excel formats. The task scheduler enables you to schedule the import and report generation, so after you have the servers and site configured, it's basically hands-off. If you don't want to purchase a third-party utility, Site Server Express is a good choice. I personally would give it a rating of 7 on a scale of 1 to 10 (with 1 being the low end and 10 being an excellent rating).

Usage Analysis

Usage Analysis is the parent of the Site Server Express log analysis tool. Usage Analysis is a component of Site Server and functions in much the same way as Site Server Express. The major differences are that you can use SQL Server as the database back end used to store the log files, and WHAT contains 45 predefined reports.

Our company was contacted by the Site Server team at Microsoft to do some stress testing of this product at one point. Microsoft provided their own hardware and software and helped get things set up initially. Just so that you have an idea of hardware recommendations, the server that Microsoft provided was a quad-processor with 512MB of RAM, and the SQL database device was set at 17GB—and this was just for log file analysis. We had configured Usage Analysis to import log files from and run reports for about 50 Web sites.

Even with the power of this server, we still found that performance was a concern. Importing the log files was not a problem, but generating the reports could take hours. One site generated log files that averaged 60–70MB per day. The import would take about one hour, but generating a report for two weeks' worth of files took more than 26 hours. However, when the process was finished, the reports were exactly what we wanted. Weighing the performance issues with the great reports, I give Usage Analysis a rating of 6 out of 10 points.

Access Watch

Access Watch is an analysis and report-generating utility that uses Perl. If you already have Perl running on your server, this is a great little program to generate some basic statistical information. It is available for download from www.accesswatch.com. After you configure the product and try it out, you can purchase a license for well less than $100.

When our company purchased Access Watch, we had it running within an hour of downloading the source files. This utility is incredibly easy to configure and gives you the basic statistics for Web site traffic. The reports are HTML pages that can be accessed from anywhere on the Internet if you have a valid account configured for accessing them. The pages include a summary of activity on the site for the specified period, the accesses for specific pages, hourly traffic, daily traffic, and a breakdown of domains and hosts. We created simple batch files and scheduled these to run with the Task Scheduler included with both Windows NT and Windows 2000. For the price and ease of use, I give Access Watch 8 out of 10 points.

WebTrends

WebTrends is an easy-to-use Windows program. It is also easy to configure and can be scheduled to import the logs and run reports. The graphical reports can be customized. WebTrends is not as fast as Access Watch when generating reports, but it is a lot faster than Usage Analysis. The interface is very basic, and setting up Web sites for reporting is a snap. Plug-ins also are available with WebTrends for use on Internet

Information Services servers. These plug-ins can be used to do reverse DNS lookups and to track cookies, which is very useful if you have Web sites that are using cookies to track users and if you prefer to see readable names rather than IP addresses.

WebTrends was our software of choice both before and after the Usage Analysis trial. However, when I upgraded to version 4.2 and started running reports, I noticed a couple blank fields. This caused errors in the reports for the number of hits to a Web site's home page. The technical support department was unfortunately not very helpful in trying to resolve the issue, forcing us to shop around for another solution. In the mean time, WebTrends released version 4.5, and the new version has resolved the issue. WebTrends can be found at `http://www.webtrends.com/`. I give it 7 out of 10 points.

Statistics Server

Statistics Server from MediaHouse Software Inc. analyzes Web site traffic in real time, so it generates Live Stats reports in a nice, simple Web interface. It includes many specialty reports and can store up to one full year of historical data that can be queried any time and in any format. In contrast to other statistics software that runs reports at a scheduled time, Statistics Server analyzes log files in near real time. The greatest benefit to this for our company is that our servers are no longer burdened for a time period once a day while the software runs the reports. This software distributes the load evenly over 24 hours. With only a few clicks of the mouse, a user can request a daily, monthly, or even yearly report for a Web site.

Statistics Server was created for marketing people and Web administrators who analyze site traffic to make sure their Internet and intranet investments work. I like it because this utility works on a single Web site or a server that hosts a few hundred Web sites. We use Statistics Server to respond to all our clients' reporting requests, instead of using different statistics software for different reports.

I recommend installing Statistics Server software on a separate computer than the Web server because it is constantly processing, and you don't want it to affect the performance of the Web sites it is analyzing. Statistics Server reads log files for different Web sites across a TCP/IP network on short, timed intervals—in our case, every six minutes. It processes Web site log files in real time and stores the resulting data in a statistics database that is much smaller than the original log files. Web site owners can then query the database from the Statistics Server HTML interface.

A few of the reasons that we have chosen Statistics Server include these:

- Web-based interface is easy to use and is accessible from nearly every Web client.

- Multiple people can concurrently access statistics for one or more Web sites.

- The utility can generate reports based on daily, weekly, or monthly time periods, or any specific length of time.

- The utility provides detailed graphs and tables.

- The Who's On feature shows who is on the Web site at that moment and what those users are accessing.

- The utility tracks inbound and outbound advertise click-throughs.
- The utility can generate a printable HTML page.

Statistics Server comes with licenses for 500 Web sites and can be used on one or more servers. We now can use the same software for all our clients, and they determine which set of statistics that they need without calling us to generate a new report and schedule it for them. You can review or purchase Statistics Server at `http://www.mediahouse.com/`. This utility deserves 9 out of 10 points.

Managing Log Files

With the 50 or so sites that are currently on one of our Web servers, log file management has become an issue. If the files are not moved off the hard drive in a timely manner, new log files will stop being generated until more disk space is made available. To avoid missing days or losing files, a simple plan can be implemented.

At the beginning of each new month, move the previous month's log files from the production Web server to a storage location. I suggest using a zip utility to reduce their size, and then storing the smaller files on a backup drive, such as a Jaz or Zip disk, or a backup tape.

One benefit of Web site statistics is that they provide a baseline for the usage of your Web sites and Web servers, and they also indicate not only when your traffic to the Web sites is increasing, but also by how much and how fast. The next chapter looks at some options for improving the performance of your Web sites and Web server.

13

Performance Tuning and Reliability

MAINTAINING A PRESENCE ON THE WEB is not only a convenience, but a necessity in today's ever-growing e-commerce market. The creation of Web sites also is more complex than ever. To create a successful Web site, you must ensure that its functionality is as impressive as its content. Therefore, in addition to creating your Web site, you should also test and monitor both your Web site and your Web server.

This chapter covers the following topics:

- The properties and options on the Performance tab of the Web Site Properties sheet

- The options available when configuring Web applications, and a detailed discussion of the Application Protection options

- Monitoring the performance of Internet Information Services and specific Web sites by using the Performance application in Windows 2000

- Improving the performance of Internet Information Services by editing the registry

- The effects of ASP pages on Internet Information Services

- Software solutions for load testing Web sites and Web servers

Optimizing Web Site Performance

The place to start when optimizing the performance of a Web site is the Performance tab of the Web Site properties sheet. Figure 13.1 displays the three options available for performance tuning each Web site.

The first two options, performance tuning and bandwidth throttling, are the same as they were in Internet Information Server 4. The Performance tuning slide bar enables you to configure Internet Information Services to expect a certain amount of Web traffic per day. As you can see in Figure 13.1, this slide bar ranges from fewer than 10,000 to more than 100,000 hits per day. Although there is one other mark in the middle of the bar, you can set the pointer at any location along the slide.

Web Site Hits

As you probably realize, the number of actual hits to your Web site is not a true indication of the number of users that access it or the amount of load that they place on the Web server. Because of this, it is not really necessary that you know how many hits per day that your Web site receives. You really need to know how much load your Web site generates in relation to the average Web site. Of course, the load generated by the average Web site is also not really a definable measure, but that is how Microsoft designed this configuration option. By default, the pointer is in the middle of the slide bar.

If you slide the pointer to the left, indicating that you receive less traffic than the average Web site, Internet Information Services will reduce the amount of memory that it allocates to the Web site. If instead you slide the pointer to the right, you indicate that

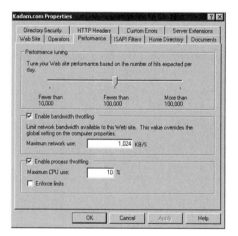

Figure 13.1   Each Web site can be individually tuned by using the Performance tab of the Web Site Properties sheet.

you receive a relatively large amount of traffic and that Internet Information Services should allocate more memory to your Web site. This memory is used to store, or cache, frequently accessed objects, such as documents and images. If the object is found in the cache, access to the object is quicker and the amount of resources needed to access the object on disk is reduced. The trade-off is that more memory is used for your Web site that could have been allocated to Windows 2000 or another resource.

Bandwidth Throttling

Bandwidth throttling enables you to limit the amount of network traffic used when accessing your site. For example, if you are billed for the amount of network traffic used by your Web site, you may want to physically limit it. Or, if you need to guarantee the availability of a portion of bandwidth for other services, you may need to limit this bandwidth.

Unless you have a limited amount of bandwidth and other more crucial services require a large portion of it, I would not recommend throttling bandwidth from within Internet Information Services. To truly utilize bandwidth throttling will inevitably mean denying data to clients who are requesting it. If your Web site is receiving more traffic than you can allocate in bandwidth, you should increase your available bandwidth.

Process Throttling

The option to specify process throttling is new in Internet Information Services 5. With process throttling, you can limit the percentage of time that the central processing unit (CPU) spends processing out-of-process applications for an individual Web site. If you run multiple Web sites on one computer, or if you have other applications running on the same computer as your Web server, process throttling ensures that processor time is available to other Web sites, non-Web applications, and the operating system. When the configured percentage of CPU time is exceeded, an event is written to the Windows 2000 Event Log.

If you require harsher consequences for applications exceeding the amount of CPU time that you allocate to them, then select the "Enforce limits" check box. This enables Level 2 and Level 3 consequences for applications that overrun their allocated processor time. With Level 2, when the processor use exceeds 150% of configured maximum CPU time, Internet Information Services will write to the Event Log and set the priority of all the out-of-process applications on that specific Web site to Idle. Setting the applications to Idle basically resets the applications and clears all resources held by them. With Level 3, when the processor use exceeds 200% of configured maximum CPU time, Internet Information Services writes to the Event Log and stops all the out-of-process applications on that Web site. Stopping the processes also releases all resources held by the applications, but requires you to manually restart them.

Running Applications

Many Web sites use Web applications to enhance the functionality of the site. In Internet Information Services, an *application* is defined as the executable files contained within a directory and its subdirectories. An application is indicated by configuring an application starting point. Web applications can include ASP code, ISAPI applications, CGI applications, DLL applications, and a collection of other options.

The application settings in Internet Information Services 5 are located on the Home Directory tab of the Web Site Properties sheet. As with Internet Information Server 4, you specify the application name, starting point, and execute permissions. The only difference here is that Permissions has been renamed Execute Permissions and is now configured using a drop-down box instead of radio buttons.

The big difference in Internet Information Services 5 is in configuring how an application is run. By default in Internet Information Server 4, almost all applications were run in the same process as the Web service. You could run one application in its own process by clicking the "Run in a separate memory space (Isolated process)" check box. In Internet Information Services 5, you now have three options that can be selected in the Application Protection drop-down box. Figure 13.2 shows the new configuration options, which are discussed next.

In Process

In the beginning, Internet Information Server only supported running all Web sites and their respective applications in one memory space. This is known as running an application *InProc*, or in the same process as the Web service. The problem with this original configuration was that when one Web application hung or failed, the entire Web server was unavailable. You had to manually restart the service—or, most likely

Figure 13.2   Web application reliability begins with choosing wisely which process to run your application.

reboot the computer—to get everything functioning again. This not only required the administrator to constantly monitor the services, but more importantly, it also required all Web sites to go offline during the computer reboot. Running applications in process is still a valid configuration in Internet Information Service 5; however, other process options make Internet Information Services much more flexible than previous versions.

Out of Process

Internet Information Server 4 made a huge advancement over its predecessors by enabling administrators to run a Web application in its own memory space. You could now isolate Web applications that may cause problems into a process that is separate from other applications and from the Web process itself. This is known as running an application *Out of Proc*, or running an application in a process separate from the Web service. If a Web application that is running in its own memory space fails, chances are good that all other Web sites will continue to function. You might be able to simply restart the WWW service of the failed Web site to restore its functionality. Even if restarting the Web service does not resolve the problem, you can schedule the reboot for a time that would not severely affect the other Web sites on the Internet Information Services server.

The drawback to running applications in their own memory space is that it requires a lot of system resources. To run a single Web application as an isolated process requires approximately 1MB of physical memory and 2MB of virtual memory. This might not seem like a big problem, but if you need to run several applications in their own memory spaces, the resources add up quickly. At a certain point, which completely depends on the amount of physical memory on your Web server, the performance of all Web sites begins to plummet. Additionally, the need for process-to-process communications affects the Web server and decreases Web site performance.

Internet Information Services 5 still supports the option of running an application in its own memory space. In some cases, isolating a potentially harmful application is well worth the resources that are required. However, at other times you might need to isolate several applications, or you might simply want to isolate all applications from the Web services. In those instances, isolating each process individually might not be a viable solution.

Pooled Out of Process

Internet Information Services 5 has again made a huge advancement by allowing one or more applications to be pooled into a separate memory space. In *Pooled Out of Proc*, one or more applications share a process that is separate from the process in which the Web service is running. As with an Out of Proc application, the Pooled Out of Proc option provides for improved reliability of the Web services. Additionally, Pooled Out of Proc reduces the memory requirements needed for the service improvement, and in turn results in better performance than when running multiple applications Out of Proc. Pooled Out of Proc is the default for all new applications configured in Internet Information Services 5. In the case of an upgrade from previous versions of Internet Information Server, applications previously configured as either InProc or Out Of Proc remain that way, but all new applications are pooled.

Internet Information Services 5 will restart the pool process after a failure. For example, suppose that you configure three applications to run in the pool. Each application is run as it is requested. Then, one of the three applications fails, which in turn fails the entire pool. When Internet Information Services receives the next request for any of the three applications in the pool, it recognizes that the pooled process is not running. Internet Information Services then restarts the pool process, and all is fine again. Most likely, only one application request receives a failure before the pool is functioning again.

Recommendations

In Internet Information Services 5, the preferred arrangement is for all applications to be run in the pool. Then, if any application fails or hangs, the Web service continues to function. However, if you have only a few applications that might cause problems, it isn't worth the risk to all the other applications to use the pooled process. In this case, it might be better to run the applications known to cause problems in isolation. Either way, Microsoft does not recommend that applications be run in the same memory space as the Web service. This is the riskiest scenario because a failure of one application could bring all of Internet Information Services to a halt.

In some instances you might want to run an application InProc. For example, if you have several applications that are not 100% stable, you should run them in the pool. But if you have a few very stable applications that you don't want to be dependent on the pool, it might be just as safe to run them InProc and save the system resources. Along those same lines, mission-critical applications should not be run in the pool because the failure of another application will cause a failure of the mission-critical application. So, although I recommend that your mission-critical applications be run Out of Proc, you might need to conserve resources and run them InProc.

Using Performance Monitor

The Windows 2000 Performance utility enables you to track various aspects of the Windows 2000 operating system and installed applications. With the Performance utility, you can gather the data needed to tune the server for optimum processing of server requests.

The Future of Pooled Processes

Internet Information Services 5 supports only one pooled process per Web site. Future versions of Internet Information Services are expected to support multiple pooled processes.

The Performance utility included with Windows 2000 has changed considerably from the Performance Monitor utility included with Windows NT 4. Probably the most important and noticeable change is the capability to monitor each Web site, or Web instance, running on the Internet Information Services. This enhancement is a result of the change in the performance counters in Internet Information Services 5.

You can also monitor the total for all Web instances, which provides the same functionality as the Performance Monitor utility in Windows NT 4. If you have only one Web site configured in Internet Information Services, then monitoring specific Web instances will not be that beneficial. However, if you host multiple Web sites on one Internet Information Services server, then having the capability to monitor an individual Web site can be a powerful tool. Monitoring individual sites allows you to determine which sites are generating the most stress on your Web server. It also allows you to troubleshoot which Web site may contain poor coding, causing the performance of your Web server to decrease. Figure 13.3 shows the new Windows 2000 Performance utility.

Another well-needed enhancement in the new Performance utility gives you the capability to allow Web site administrators to view performance statistics for their Web site. Because the Performance utility is now an MMC snap-in, you can create MMC modules for individual Web sites and grant access to those modules to the Web site administrator or developer for that site. This allows an administrator or developer to view and evaluate the performance counters for a specific Web site, but does not allow this information to be viewed for other Web sites on a shared Web server.

When your Web server is up and running, you should monitor it for performance issues. First, monitor the server to find a performance baseline. For baselines on our servers, I turn on logging and monitor key counters for one weekday. You may choose a different timeframe based on the usage of your Web site. Then, as your site grows, your users increase, or your hardware changes, you can compare the new performance statistics to those measured in your baseline. This tells you how much things have changed and helps you plan for future expansions.

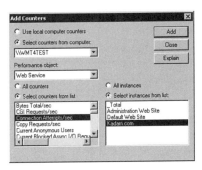

Figure 13.3 The Windows 2000 Performance utility provides the much-needed feature of monitoring a specific Web site in addition to monitoring all Web sites as a group.

When monitoring and optimizing your Web server, you will probably want to look at four objects: Internet Information Services Global, Web Service, FTP Service, and Active Server Pages.

Internet Information Services Global

The Internet Information Services Global object is used to measure the overall settings in Internet Information Services. The default counter in the Internet Information Services Global object is `Total Rejected Async I/O Requests`. This counter enables you to track the total number of rejected requests due to bandwidth throttling techniques. It is important to note that this counter will keep track of these requests from the time Internet Information Services is started. To clear this particular counter, you must stop and start Internet Information Services or reboot the server. If you are not using bandwidth throttling, this counter will not be of any value to you.

One of the counters that I use is `BLOB Cache Hits %`. Internet Information Services uses a portion of server memory to cache frequently accessed objects, as discussed previously in the "Web Site Hits" section. This cache improves the performance of the Web server by retrieving Binary Large Objects (BLOBs), such as graphical images, from memory rather than accessing the hard drive. If you see a decrease in this counter over time, you should add physical memory to your Web server to increase the size of the cache in response to the increase in object requests.

Web Service

The default Web Service counter—and the most useful one to the Web administrator—is `Bytes Total/sec`. This counter provides you the total number of bytes sent and received by all Web sites or a specific Web site. You can use this counter to determine which Web site is generating the most network traffic on your Web server and then follow the increase or decrease in total network traffic to your Web server. This is an excellent tool to help you plan for hardware upgrades to your Web server.

FTP Service

The FTP Service object has counters very similar to the counters found in the Web Service object. So, again, one of the more important counters is `Bytes Total/sec`. In this case, this counter measures the traffic for the same objects as the Web service counter, but only as they are accessed by using FTP.

Active Server Pages

With the increase of ASP content in today's Web sites, the Active Server Pages object is one of the more important objects. It can provide information on the usage of ASP code and also can assist in troubleshooting both code problems and performance issues. The Active Server Pages counter that can be of most use is `Debugging`

`Requests`. This counter tracks the number of debugging documents requested by Internet Information Services. If this number is high, then the number of scripting errors in the ASP content is high, although this could indicate that a few poorly coded pages are receiving a lot of requests. Low numbers relate to low errors and indicate good coding.

You should also examine the global memory available. This may pick up on errors that would not normally be found through the Web services, such as ADO connections not being destroyed and other memory leaks.

Editing the Registry to Improve Performance

Editing the registry settings in Windows NT 4 was sometimes the best and only way to improve the performance of Internet Information Server 4. With Internet Information Services 5, I expect that, on occasion, the same will hold true. Because Internet Information Services 5 is deployed in more environments, administrators will find new issues and Microsoft will respond with new modifications for the registry.

Improving ASP Functionality

As discussed in Chapter 7, "Running Web Applications," Active Server Pages (ASP) are a way of combining scripting code with other Web objects. However, unlike typical Java code, ASP pages include *server-side code*. That is, the code in an ASP page is executed in the memory space of the Internet Information Services. The results are then sent to the browser client as static Hypertext Markup Language (HTML) code.

Because the code in an ASP page is executed on the Internet Information Services server, it requires resources on that computer, including memory, pointers, and threads. I want to emphasize this point because of the importance ASP plays in the performance of Internet Information Services. Even if you took a static Web page authored entirely in HTML and simply renamed the page with an `.asp` extension, the page would load slower that the same Web page with an `.htm` extension.

Other considerations for improving performance of your ASP pages include using application state for caching output, enabling buffering for all applications, disabling session state if it is not needed, and using `OptionExplicit` with VBScript.

Load Testing

All Web administrators want their sites to run correctly and efficiently, and most Web administrators take a lot of time and effort to ensure that this happens. First, the Web site is tested thoroughly for functionality, and then Internet Information Services is

> **More Counters and Objects**
>
> The counters and objects discussed in this chapter are just a few of those available in the Windows 2000 Performance utility. For a more thorough explanation of the counters or processes, refer to the online help, the Internet Information Services 5 Resource Kit, and the Windows 2000 Resource Kit.

optimized. Any applications are configured to run optimally. Finally, the Web site is ready for the Internet. But, sometimes that just isn't enough. I have seen a Web master do everything listed, and probably more, and then have his Web site fail within a week. Why? Because his site was too successful, and the thousands of requests every minute for his ASP pages was more than his Web server could manage.

Load testing is the only way to prevent such a tragedy. In load testing, typically a third-party application simulates thousands of users accessing the site at once. Some companies even choose to place their Web site on the Internet with no testing at all. Well, it will be load tested, but the company might not have wanted the results to be so public. The results of load testing can range from a list of broken links to the entire failure of the Web service. Often, though, the results lay somewhere in the middle. Maybe you'll discover the maximum number of requests that your Web site can manage at one time, or you'll find that you should adjust a configuration option. Whatever the results, the goal is the same: to guarantee the availability of the Web site.

Load testing of your Web server is not a necessity; however, if you administer multiple Web sites on one Internet Information Services server, or if you expect a significant amount of traffic to your Web site, it might be cost-effective to test your Web site and Web server for load capacities and deficiencies in the coding. After all, it is not the products or services you sell that can make your Web site successful on the Internet; it is the amount of traffic that your Web site receives and how much of that traffic is capable of finding what's needed while at your Web site.

The simplest load testing method is to do it manually. This method requires a company to gather together numerous people and have them all access the Web site at the same time and in a similar manner in an attempt to test a server and a Web site under a heavy load. The problem with this method is that it can be very difficult to find enough people to really put a load on a Web server. It can also be unmanageable and very costly to pay people to sit and push buttons and click a mouse in an attempt to overload a Web server. Many companies turn to testing labs that specialize in this field. However, with the convenience of a testing lab also comes the cost of using its services.

Another method of testing a Web site and the underlying Web server is through the use of an Automated Software Quality (ASQ) tool. ASQ tools test a Web site and Web server by automating the testing process. Software programs run scripts that simulate hundreds of simultaneous connections and push the server to its limits. In most cases, the software tracks the test through graphs and reports that enable the tester to easily interpret the data. Automated testing is more efficient that manual testing in improving the quality and functionality of a Web site.

The remainder of this section discusses several load-testing tools: WebLoad 3.0, Microsoft Web Capacity Analysis Tool, and the Microsoft HTTPMon Utility.

WebLoad 3.5

One example of automated load-testing software is WebLoad 3.5, by RadView Software, Inc. WebLoad executes user-created test scripts and monitors the performance response of the Web application, including transactions per second (TPS), response time, and throughput. This method allows WebLoad to focus on Web scalability testing and the responsiveness of Web applications. Testing the responsiveness of Web applications is key in verifying the productiveness of mission-critical applications such as those associated with many e-commerce sites. A trial version is included with the Visual InterDev Web Solutions Kit. I like WebLoad 3.5 because it provides all the features that a Web administrator should need in a load-testing solution.

Microsoft Web Capacity Analysis Tool

The Microsoft Web Capacity Analysis Tool (WCAT) runs simulated workloads on a Web server. WCAT is specially designed to evaluate how Web servers running Internet Information Services respond to various client workload simulations by using virtual clients. Using WCAT, you can test how Internet Information Services responds to multiple client requests, or you can test varying configurations of the server. WCAT can also test the responsiveness of your network configuration. The results of these tests can be used to determine the optimal server and network configuration in which to run Internet Information Services. In contrast to most third-party applications, WCAT is inexpensive because it is included on Microsoft TechNet and in the Microsoft Windows 2000 Resource Kit.

To use WCAT, you must first copy and remove DLLs and then start and stop the World Wide Web Publishing Service. When the server is ready to test, you can then use one of the prepared test workloads included with WCAT, or you can create your own workload. WCAT also includes a special option that adds Secure Sockets Layer (SSL) protocol settings to any workload test. For detailed instructions on how to configure and use WCAT, refer to the Microsoft Windows 2000 Resource Kit. I think WCAT is a little more complicated to use than WebLoad 3.5, but, again, it provides everything you should need to evaluate the performance of your Web server.

Microsoft HTTPMon Utility

HTTPMon is a browser-based tool used to monitor the activity and performance of Web sites and Web servers. It was developed by the employees at Microsoft who manage the company's Web site. By emulating the way that users attempt to connect to a Web site, HTTPMon is capable of ensuring the availability of a server connection and aiding in avoiding servers that are unavailable. It is designed to use existing pages on a specific Web server to capture user experiences and translate them into a type of performance analysis. This utility can be simultaneously run on multiple servers to test connectivity and to display connectivity statistics.

HTTPMon works as a multithread process operating with the values and within the limits that you set in its HTTPMon.ini file. These limits specify which Web site is tested, the number of times it is tested, and the frequency with which you can retry a failed connection before moving on to the next configured site. You can also configure additional parameters that optimize HTTPMon to your installation, such as setting a maximum thread pool count and configuring the output file and location. The results of the test are written to a standard common-separated value (CSV) file that can then be examined by or imported into a variety of tools, including Microsoft Excel and Microsoft SQL Server. For detailed instructions on how to configure and use HTTPMon, refer to the Microsoft Internet Information Services 5 Resource Kit. If you want to customize every detail of your load-testing tool, then HTTPMon is an excellent solution for you.

This chapter has given you a place to begin when optimizing your Internet Information Services server. As time goes on, Microsoft and Web administrators will find new ways of improving the performance of the Web server and the Web sites that it houses. Look for this new information in books, chat rooms, and Web sites, and share what you have learned with others.

Index

Symbols

* (asterisks), Password Box, 76

40-bit encryption, 104

128-bit encryption, 104

A

Access, SQL Server database compared, 131

access control
described, 36
methods of, 41

access control lists (ACLs), 28, 99

"Access Denied" error message, 30

"Access Forbidden" error message, 30

access permissions
directory browsing permission, 41
execute permissions, 41
IIS security, 39-41
read access permission, 40
script source permission, 41
write permission, 40

Access tab, SMTP site properties, 118

access tokens, Windows 2000 security, 29-30

Access Watch, 139

account operators, 58-59

ACLs (access control lists), 28, 99

Active Server Pages (ASP). *See* ASP (Active Server Pages)

Active Server Pages object, 150

administration
browser-based ISM, 9
MMC (Microsoft Management Console), 8-9
remote administration, 9
third-party options, 9

ADO (ActiveX Data Objects), 124-125

anonymous access, 42, 100

anonymous user accounts, FTP service, 74

App Debugging property sheet, 90-91

App Mappings property sheet, 88-89

App Options property sheet, 89-90

Application Protection drop-down box, 88

.asp file extension, 85

ASP (Active Server Pages), 82, 85-86
advantages of, 86
App Options property sheet and, 89-90
disadvantages of, 87
enabling, 86
Jscript, 85
performance issues, 151
scripting languages, 85-86
VBScript, 85

AspMail, 115

asterisks (*), Password Box, 76

auditing, 33

authentication
anonymous access, 42
basic authentication, 44-45
CA (Certificate Authority), 108-109
challenge numbers, 44
digest authentication, 45
encryption compared, 104
Fortezza authentication, 46
FTP service, anonymous access, 42
IIS security, 41-42, 48
integrated Windows authentication, 43-44
Netscape Navigator clients, 45
selecting an authentication method, 46-47
with SSL, 106

B

backup strategies, 10
bandwidth allocation, cages, 14
bandwidth throttling, 145
basic authentication, 44-45, 100
BIG/ip (F5 Labs), 22
BLOBs (Binary Large Objects), 150

C

CA (Certificate Authority), 108-109
CA certificates, 108
cages, 13-14
capacity planning, 18
content replication, 23
Microsoft Content Replication System (CRS), 24
Windows 2000 Replicaton Service, 24
fault tolerance, 20-21
hardware solutions, 21
BIG/ip (F5 Labs), 22
DistributedDirector (Cisco), 22
LocalDirector (Cisco), 21-22

load balancing, 20
software solutions, 22
Loadbal, 22
Microsoft Cluster Server, 23
Network Load Balancing (NLB), 23
system monitoring, 18-19
Enterprise Monitor, 19-20
WhatsUp Gold, 19
CDO (Collaboration Data Object), 115-116
Certificate Authority (CA), 108-109
certificate mapping, 106
certificate wildcard mapping, 109
Certification Authority Server, 110-112
CGI (Common Gateway Interface), 82
challenge numbers, 44
client certificate mapping, 105
certificate mapping, 106
Fortezza cards, 106
many-to-one mapping, 105-106
one-to-one mapping, 105-106
selection of mapping method, 107
types of, 105
client certificates
described, 105
distributing, 109-110
clustering, 21
co-location servers, 13
Collaboration Data Object (CDO), 115-116
Common Gateway Interface (CGI), 82
content organization, 6
considerations for, 6
FrontPage Server Extensions, 6
hard drives, 6-7
Virtual Server, 6

content replication, 23
  Microsoft Content Replication System
    (CRS), 24
  Windows 2000 Replication
    Service, 24

**CRS (Microsoft Content Replication
System), 24**

Current Sessions node, 115

Custom installation, 8

D

data centers, 13–14

data source failures, 129

Data Source Name (DSN), 126

database connectivity
  Access database versus SQL server
    database, 131
  background, 123
  Data Source Name (DSN), 126
  drivers, 127
  DSN-less connections, 130
  File DSN, 130
  MDAC, 124
    *ADO (ActiveX Data Objects),
      124-125*
    *ODBC (Open Database
      Connectivity), 126*
    OLE DB, 125-126
    version checking, 131-132
  name of database, 126
  on-the-fly DSN, 130
  passwords, 127
  pre-connection issues, 126–127
  security issues, 132
  servers, 126
  SQL Server, 131
  System DSN, 127–129
  user ID, 127

dedicated servers, 13

default directories
  FrontPage Server Extensions, 96
  SMTP, 115

**delivery options, SMTP site
properties, 118**

digest authentication, 45

digital certificates, 106–107

directories
  NNTP, 120
  SMTP, 115

directory browsing permission, 41

**directory listing style, FTP sites,
78–79**

disk mirroring, 3

DistributedDirector (Cisco), 22

DNS configuration, 14–15
  DNS Round Robin, 16–18
  domain registration, 15
  subdomains, 16

DNS Round Robin, 16–18

domain controller, 7

domain names
  assigning, 56
  restrictions, 37
    group of computers, 38
    single computer, 37-38
    single domain, 38-39

domain registration, 15

domains, configuring SMTP, 119

Domains node, 115

Drivers, database connectivity, 127

DSN (Data Source Name), 126

DSN-less connections, 130

dynamic content, 85

E

encryption, 104
  40-bit encryption, 104
  128-bit encryption, 104
  authentication compared, 104
  server certificates, 105

Enterprise Monitor, 19-20

error messages, 30

Everyone special group,
  Windows 2000 security, 33

execute permissions, 41

Execute Permissions drop-down
  list, 88

F

fault tolerance, 20-21

File DSN, 130

file extensions, Web applications, 82

File Transfer Protocol (FTP). *See*
  FTP (File Transfer Protocol)

Fortezza authentication, 46

Fortezza cards, 106

Fpremadm utility, 98-99

Fpsrvadm utility, 98

Fpsrvadm.exe, 95

FQDN (Fully Qualified Domain
  Name), 14

FreeWAIS, 102

FrontPage
  FreeWAIS, 102
  indexing services, 102
  integration with other services,
    101-102
  virtual directories and, 58
  web sites
    browsing, 100
    enhancing, 101
    publishing, 101

Frontpage 2000 Server Extensions,
  SMTP, 116

FrontPage 2000 Server Extensions
  Resource Kit (SERK), 96

FrontPage Server Extensions,
  66-67, 93
  ACLs (access control lists), 99
  administration of, 98-99
    Fpremadm utility, 98-99
    HTML Administration Forms, 98
    Server Extensions snap-in
      (to MMC), 98
    Windows Scripting Host (WSH), 99
  administrative tools, installing, 95
  backward compatibility, 94
  browse-time components, 100-101
  components, installing, 95
  configuring, 97-98
  content organization, 6
  default directories, 96
  Fpsrvadm.exe, 95
  installing, 94-96
    administratitive tools, 95
    components, 95
    default directories, 96
    FrontPage 2000 Server Extensions
      Resource Kit (SERK), 96
    postinfo.html, 96
    vti inf.html, 96
  Internet Information Server 4, 97
  security issues, 99
    ACLs, 99
    anonymous access, 100
    authentication of users, 99-100
    basic authentication, 100
    Integrated Windows
      authentication, 100
  SMTP agents, 102
  users and, 100, 101
  virtual servers, extending, 97

FTP (File Transfer Protocol), 69
  account synchronization, 75
  anonymous users, 74

architecture of, 70-71
authentication, anonymous access, 42
Internet Information Server 3, 73
Internet Information Services
  Metabase, 72
IP addresses, 71-72
multiple FTP sites, 73
nonanonymous users, 74-75
ports, 73
security accounts, 73
  account synchronization, 75
  anonymous users, 74
  nonanonymous users, 74-75
Services file, 72
site properties, 71-72
TCP as transport protocol for, 70-71
TCP ports, 72

**FTP service, NetBIOS
connection, 77**

FTP Service object, 150

FTP sites
creating, 80
home directory, 76
  access permissions, 78
  directory listing style, 78-79
  local directories, 76
  remote directories, 76-78
NTFS permissions, 78

FTP virtual directories, 79

FTP virtual servers, 71-72

**Fully Qualified Domain Name
(FQDN), 14**

G-H

**General tab, SMTP site
properties, 117**

**global configuration, Web
applications, 83**

global.asa file, 85

**group accounts, Windows 2000
security, 28**

hackers, IIS security, 39

hard drives
content organization, 6-7
optimal configuration, 4
system requirements, 3

hits, Web site, 144-145

home directory, 59-60
FTP sites, 76
  access permissions, 78
  directory listing style, 78-79
  local directories, 76
  remote directories, 76-78
local home directory, 60, 62
remote home directory, 60-62
URL redirection, 62

host headers, 62-63
adding, 65
advantages of, 66
disadvantages of, 65-66
HTTP 1.1, 63-64
  HTTP DELETE, 65
  HTTP PUT, 65
  persistent connections, 64
  pipelining, 64
limitations of, 63

host name configuration, 14

**hosting companies, selection of,
12-13**

Hosting options, 12

HTML Administration Forms, 98

**HTTP (HyperText Transfer
Protocol), 52**

**HTTP 1.1 (Hypertext Transfer
Protocol version 1.1), 63-64**
features of, 64
HTTP DELETE, 65
HTTP PUT, 65
persistent conections, 64
pipelining, 64

HTTP communication, 52

HTTP DELETE, 65

HTTP keepalives, 64

HTTPMon utility, 153

HyperText Transfer Protocol version 1.1. *See* **HTTP 1.1 (Hypertext Transfer Protocol version 1.1)**

I-J

IIS security, 35, 37
 access control
  described, 36
  methods of, 41
 access permissions, 39–41
  directory browsing permission, 41
  execute permissions, 41
  read access permission, 40
  script source permission, 41
  write permission, 40
 anonymous access, 42
 authentication, 41–42
  anonymous access, 42
  basic authentication, 44–45
  challenge numbers, 44
  digest authentication, 45
  Fortezza authentication, 46
  integrated Windows authentication, 43-44
  methods, 48
  selecting an authentication method, 46-47
 basic authentication, 44–45
 challenge numbers, 44
 digest authentication, 45
 directory browsing permission, 41
 domain name restrictions, 37–39
 execute permissions, 41
 Fortezza authentication, 46
 hackers, 39
 impersonation, 47–48
 integrated Windows authentication, 43–44

 IP address restrictions, 37–39
 NTFS permissions, 40
 read access permission, 40
 script source permission, 41
 subauthentication DLL, 47
 Windows 2000 security and, 26
 write permission, 40

impersonation, 47-48

in-process configuration (Web applications), 146, 148

indexing services, 102

InetPub directory, 6

InProc, 146, 148

installation, 7
 Certification Authority Server, 110–112
 content organization, 6–7
 Custom installation, 8
 pre-installation issues, 2
 security configuration, 5
 steps for, 8
 system requirements, 2
  hardware, 2, 4
  software, 5

integrated Windows authentication, 43–44, 100

Internet Information Server 3, FTP (File Transfer Protocol), 73

Internet Information Services Global, 150

Internet Information Services Metabase, 72

Internet Server Application Programming Interface (ISAPI), 82, 84–85

Internet Service Manager (ISM), 9

internetworking, 11
 capacity planning, 18
 co-location servers, 13
 data centers, 13–14

dedicated servers, 13
DNS configuration, 14-15
domain registration, 15
host name configuration, 14
Hosting options, 12
Shared servers, 12-13
subdomains, 16

intranets, virtual directories, 57

IP addresses
All Unassigned option, 55, 71-72
assigning, 55-56
number of, 55
restrictions, 37
group of computers, 38
single computer, 37-38
single domain, 38-39
virtual servers, 55-56

**ISAPI (Internet Server Application
Programming Interface), 82, 84-85**

ISM (Internet Service Manager), 9

IUSR computername accounts, 74
auditing and logging, 33
passwords, 28, 43

Jscript, 85

K-L

**LDAP routing, SMTP site
properties, 119**

load balancing, 20

load testing
described, 151-152
HTTPMon utility, 153-154
WCAT (Web Capacity Analysis
Tool), 153
WebLoad 3.5, 152

Loadbal, 22

local home directory, 60, 62

LocalDirector (Cisco), 21-22

log files
Access Watch, 139
Date field, 136
described, 133-134
formats
Microsoft IIS Log File Format, 134
NCSA format, 135
ODBC logging, 135-136
W3C Extended Log File Format,
136-137
frequency of generating reports, 134
generating reports, 134, 137
Access Watch, 139
frequency of, 134
Site Server Express, 138
Statistics Server, 140-141
Usage Analysis, 139
WebTrends, 139-140
managing, 141
Microsoft IIS Log File Format, 134
NCSA format, 135
ODBC logging, 135-136
Site Server Express, 138
size limits, 134
Statistics Server, 140-141
Usage Analysis, 139
W3C Extended Log File Format,
136-137
WebTrends, 139-140

**logging access, Windows 2000
security, 33**

**logon rights, Windows 2000
security, 29**

M

**mass media devices, system
requirements, 4**

**MDAC (Microsoft Data Access
Components)**
ADO (ActiveX Data Objects),
124-125
described, 124

ODBC (Open Database
Connectivity), 126
OLE DB, 125-126
version checking, 131-132

**messages options, SMTP site
properties, 118**

Microsoft Cluster Server, 23

**Microsoft Content Replication
System (CRS), 24**

Microsoft Data Access Components.
See **MDAC (Microsoft Data Access
Components)**

Microsoft Exchange, 117

Microsoft IIS Log File Format, 134

**Microsoft Management Console
(MMC), 8-9**

Microsoft Security Web Site, 34

**Microsoft Windows Update
option, 132**

**MIME (Multipurpose Internet Mail
Extension), 84**

**MMC (Microsoft Management
Console), 8-9**

Monitors, system requirements, 3

**MTS (Microsoft Transaction
Server), 83**

**Multipurpose Internet Mail
Extension (MIME), 84**

N

NCSA log file format, 135

NetBIOS, FTP service, 77

**Netscape Navigator,
authentication, 45**

**Network interface card (NIC),
system requirements, 3**

Network Load Balancing (NLB), 23

**Network News Transport Protocol
(NNTP).** *See* **NNTP (Network
News Transport Protocol)**

Newmail object, 116

**NNTP (Network News Transport
Protocol)**
described, 119
directories, 120
process, 120
services, 120-121

nodes, SMTP, 114
Current Sessions node, 115
Domains node, 115

**nonanonymous user accounts, FTP
service, 74-75**

NTFS (NT file system)
configuration, sample, 32
permissions, 31-32, 40, 78
Windows 2000 security, 30-32
configuration, sample, 32
permissions, 31-32
user accounts, 28

O

**ODBC (Open Database
Connectivity), 126**

ODBC log file format, 135-136

OLE DB, 125-126

**on-the-fly DSN, database
connectivity, 130**

Onstream ADR tape drive, 4

**Open Database Connectivity
(ODBC), 126**

operators, 58-59

Out of Proc, 147

**out-of-process configuration (Web
applications), 147**

P

passwords
  asterisks in Password Box, 76
  database connectivity, 127
  FTP account synchronization, 75
  IUSR computername account, 28, 43
  Windows 2000 security, 28

pcANYWHERE, 9

per site configuration, Web applications, 83

performance issues
  ASP functionality, 151
  load testing
    described, 151-152
    HTTPMon utility, 153-154
    WCAT (Web Capacity Analysis Tool), 153
    WebLoad 3.5, 152
  registry settings, editing, 151
  Web applications
    in-process configuration, 146
    out-of-process configuration, 147
    pooled out-of-process configuration, 147-148
    recommendations for, 148
  Web sites
    bandwidth throttling, 145
    described, 144
    hits, 144-145
    process throttling, 145
  Windows 2000 Performance utility. *See* Windows 2000 Performance utility

Perl scripts, 82

permissions
  access permissions, 39-41
    directory browsing permission, 41
    execute permissions, 41
    read access permission, 40
    script source permission, 41
    write permission, 40
  Everyone permissions, removing, 5
  FTP sites, 78
  NTFS permissions, 31-32

persistent connections, 64

physical directories
  described, 56-57
  virtual directories, sharing name with, 58

physical servers, 54

pipelining, 64

pooled out-of-process configuration (Web applications), 147-148

pooled processes
  future trends, 148
  Pooled Out of Proc option, 147-148
  situations for, 148

Post.Office, 117

postinfo.html, 96

pre-installation issues, 2

process throttling, 145

processors, system requirements, 3

Q-R

racks, 13-14

RAID 5, system requirements, 3-4

read access permission, 40

redirect variables, 62

registry settings, editing, 151

remote administration, 9

remote home directory, 60-62

RFC compliance, SMTP, 114

root certificates
  described, 108
  adding, 109

root directory, Web applications, 82

Root Web, 97

S-T

script source permission, 41

SCSI drives, system requirements, 4

Secure Sockets Layer. *See* **SSL (Secure Sockets Layer)**

security
   anonymous access, 100
   authentication
      anonymous access, 42
      basic authentication, 44-45
      CA (Certificate Authority), 108-109
      challenge numbers, 44
      digest authentication, 45
      encryption compared, 104
      Fortezza authentication, 46
      FTP service, anonymous access, 42
      IIS security, 41-42, 48
      integrated Windows authentication, 43-44
      Netscape Navigator clients, 45
      selecting an authentication method, 46-47
      with SSL, 106
   basic authentication, 100
   client certificate mapping, 105
      certificate mapping, 106
      Fortezza cards, 106
      many-to-one mapping, 105-106
      one-to-one mapping, 105-106
      selection of mapping method, 107
      types of, 105
   client certificates
      described, 105
      distributing, 109-110
   database connectivity, 132
   encryption
      40-bit encryption, 104
      128-bit encryption, 104
      authentication compared, 104
      server certificates, 105
   Everyone permissions, removing, 5
   FrontPage Server Extensions, 99
   FTP service, 73
      account synchronization, 75
      anonymous users, 74
      nonanonymous users, 74-75
   Integrated Windows authentication, 100
   preliminary steps, 5
   remote home directory, 61
   server certificates
      described, 108
      authenticating, 108-109
   SGC (Server-Gated Cryptography), 104
   SSL (Secure Sockets Layer). *See* SSL (Secure Sockets Layer)
   unnecessary Windows 2000 services, disabling, 5-6
   user authentication, FrontPage Server Extensions, 99-100
   virtual directories, 57
   Windows 2000 security. *See* Windows 2000 security
   X.509 digital certificates, 106-107

Security tab, SMTP site properties, 119

SendMail components, 115
   CDO, 115-116
   Frontpage 2000 Server Extensions, 116

SERK (FrontPage 2000 Server Extensions Resource Kit), 96

server certificates
   described, 105, 108
   authenticating, 108-109

Server-Gated Cryptography (SGC), 104

servers, database connectivity, 126

Services file, 72

SGC (Server-Gated Cryptography), 104

shared servers
  advantages of, 12
  hosting company selection, 12-13
  virtual servers, 12

Simple Mail Transfer Protocol.
  See **SMTP (Simple Mail Transfer Protocol)**

Site Server Express, 138

sites (Web). *See* **Web sites**

SMTP (Simple Mail Transfer Protocol)
  default directories, 115
  delivery errors, 116
  described, 113-114
  domains, configuring, 119
  Newmail object, 116
  nodes, 114
    Current Sessions node, 115
    Domains node, 115
  RFC compliance, 114
  SendMail components, 115
    CDO, 115-116
    FrontPage 2000 Server Extensions, 116
  site properties, 117
    Access tab, 118
    delivery options, 118
    General tab, 117
    LDAP routing, 119
    messages options, 118
    Security tab, 119
  spam, restricting, 119
  third-party options, 117

SMTP agents, 102

software, system requirements, 5

spam, 119

SQL Server, 131

SSL (Secure Sockets Layer), 103
  adding, 47
  authentication, 106

  encryption
    server certificates, 105
    SGC (Server-Gated Cryptography), 104

starting-point directory, Web applications, 82

static content, 85

Statistics Server, 140-141

subauthentication DLL, 47

subdomains, 16

subwebs, 97
  creating, 98
  extending, 98

System DSN, 127-129

system monitoring, 18-19
  Enterprise Monitor, 19-20
  WhatsUp Gold, 19

system requirements
  hardware, 2, 4
    hard drives, 3
    mass media devices, 4
    monitors, 3
    Network interface card (NIC), 3
    processors, 3
    RAID 5, 3-4
    SCSI drives, 4
    video cards, 3
  installation, 2
  software, 4

TCP (Transmission Control Protocol), 70, 72

top level domain (TLD) servers, 15

Transmission Control Protocol (TCP), 70, 72

troubleshooting, Windows 2000 security, 32-33

U-V

URLs (uniform resource locators)
components of, 52-53
redirect variables, 62
redirection, 62

Usage Analysis, 139

user accounts, Windows 2000 security, 27-28
access tokens, 29-30
logon rights, 29
passwords, 28

user ID, database connectivity, 127

VBScript, 85

video cards, system requirements, 3

virtual directories, 57-58
FrontPage and, 58
FTP virtual directories, 79
intranets, 57
limitations , 58
physical directories, sharing name with, 58
security, 57

Virtual Server, content organization, 6

virtual servers, 12, 54
domain names, assigning, 56
extending, 97
FrontPage Server Extensions, installing, 97
IP addresses, assigning, 55-56
Root Web, 97
subwebs, 97

vti inf.html, 96

W-Z

W3C Extended Log File Format, 136-137

WAM (Web Application Manager), 83-84

WCAT (Web Capacity Analysis Tool), 153

Web Application Manager (WAM), 83-84

Web applications, 81-82, 146
App Options property sheet, 89-90
ASP (Active Server Pages). *See* ASP (Active Server Pages)
CGI (Common Gateway Interface), 82
configuration, 83
creating, 87-88
App Debugging property sheet, 90
App Mappings property sheet, 88
App Options property sheet, 89-90
customizing, 87-88
file extensions, 82
global configuration, 83
in process, 146, 148
ISAPI applications, 82, 84-85
MIME (Multipurpose Internet Mail Extension), 84
out of process, 147
per site configuration, 83
Perl scripts, 82
pooled out of process, 147-148
recommendations for, 148
root directory, 82
starting-point directory, 82
WAM (Web Application Manager), 83-84

Web Capacity Analysis Tool (WCAT), 153

Web servers, performance monitoring
Active Server Pages object, 150
described, 149-150
FTP Service object, 150
Internet Information Services Global object, 150
Web Service object, 150

Web Service object, 150

Web sites, 51
   accessing, Web client steps for, 53
   applications, running, 146
      in process, 146, 148
      out of process, 147
      pooled out of process, 147-148
      recommendations for, 148
   bandwidth throttling, 145
   browsing, 100
   domain names, assigning, 56
   enhancing, 101
   hits, 144-145
   home directory, 59-60
      local home directory, 60
      remote home directory, 60-62
      URL redirection, 62
   host headers, 62-63
      adding, 65
      advantages of, 66
      disadvantages of, 65-66
      HTTP 1.1, 63-64
   IP addresses, assigning, 55-56
   operators, 58-59
   organizational structures, 53
      physical directories, 56-57
      physical servers, 54
      virtual directories, 57-58
      virtual servers, 54
   performance, optimizing, 144
      applications, 146
      bandwidth throttling, 145
      process throttling, 145
      Web site hits, 144-145
   process throttling, 145
   publishing, 101
   server extensions, 66-67
   Windows 2000 Performance utility.
      See Windows 2000 Performance
      utility
WebLoad 3.5, 152
WebTrends, 139-140
WhatsUp Gold, 19
wildcard certificates, 109
Windows 2000, Microsoft Windows
  Update option, 132

Windows 2000 Performance
  utility, 151
   Active Server Pages object, 150
   described, 148-149
   Internet Information Services Global
      object, 150
   Web server performance monitoring
      Active Server Pages object, 150
      FTP Service object, 150
      Internet Information Services Global
        object, 150
      Web Service object, 150
Windows 2000 Replication
  Service, 24
Windows 2000 security, 25-26
   auditing, 33
   Everyone special group, 33
   group accounts, 28
   IIS directories, 34
   IIS security and, 26
   IUSR computername account, 33
   logging access, 33
   NTFS, 30-32
      configuration, sample, 32
      permissions, 31-32
   planning, 34
   recommendations, 27
   troubleshooting , 32-33
   user accounts, 27-28
      access control lists (ACLs), 28
      access tokens, 29-30
      logon rights, 29
      NTFS, 28
      passwords, 28
Windows Scripting Host (WSH), 99
Windows Sockets API, 52
WinSock, 52
World Wide Web Consortium, 53
write permission, 40
WSH (Windows Scripting Host), 99
WWWRoot directory, 6
X.509 digital certificates, 106-107

 # How to Contact Us

Visit Our Web Site

`www.newriders.com`

On our Web site you'll find information about our other books, authors, tables of contents, indexes, and book errata.

Email Us

Contact us at this address:

`newriders@mcp.com`

- If you have comments or questions about this book
- To report errors that you have found in this book
- If you have a book proposal to submit or are interested in writing for New Riders
- If you would like to have an author kit sent to you
- If you are an expert in a computer topic or technology and are interested in being a technical editor who reviews manuscripts for technical accuracy

`newriders@mcp.com`

- To find a distributor in your area, please contact our international department at this address.

`nrmedia@mcp.com`

- For instructors from educational institutions who wish to preview New Riders books for classroom use. Email should include your name, title, school, department, address, phone number, office days/hours, text in use, and enrollment in the body of your text, along with your request for desk/examination copies and/or additional information.

Write to Us

New Riders Publishing

201 W. 103rd St.

Indianapolis, IN 46290-1097

Call Us

Toll-free (800) 571-5840 + 9 +4511

If outside U.S. (317) 581-3500. Ask for New Riders.

Fax Us

(317) 581-4663

Windows 2000 Answers

Updated edition of New Riders' best-selling *Inside Windows NT 4 Server*. Taking the author-driven, no-nonsense approach we pioneered with our Windows NT *Landmark* books, New Riders proudly offers something unique for Windows 2000 administrators—an interesting and discriminating book on Windows 2000 Server, written by someone in the trenches who can anticipate your situation and provide answers you can trust.

**INSIDE
Windows 2000
Server**

ISBN: 1-56205-929-7

Architected to be the most navigable, useful, and value-packed reference for Windows 2000, this book uses a creative "telescoping" design that you can adapt to your style of learning. Written by Steven Tate, key Windows 2000 partner and developer of Microsoft's W2K Training Program, it's a concise, focused quick reference for Windows 2000.

ISBN: 0-7357-0869-X

Windows 2000 Active Directory is just one of several new Windows 2000 titles from New Riders' acclaimed *Landmark* series. Focused advice on planning, implementing, and managing the Active Directory in your business.

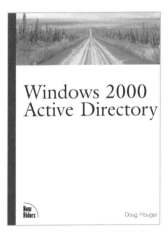

**Windows 2000
Active Directory**

Doug Hauger

ISBN: 0-7357-0870-3

Advanced Information on Networking Technologies

New Riders Books Offer Advice and Experience

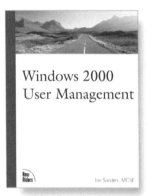

LANDMARK

Rethinking Computer Books

We know how important it is to have access to detailed, solutions-oriented information on core technologies. *Landmark* books contain the essential information you need to solve technical problems. Written by experts and subjected to rigorous peer and technical reviews, our *Landmark* books are hard-core resources for practitioners like you.

ESSENTIAL REFERENCE

Smart, Like You

The *Essential Reference* series from New Riders provides answers when you know what you want to do but need to know how to do it. Each title skips extraneous material and assumes a strong base of knowledge. These are indispensable books for the practitioner who wants to find specific features of a technology quickly and efficiently. Avoiding fluff and basic material, these books present solutions in an innovative, clean format—and at a great value.

MCSE CERTIFICATION

Engineered for Test Success

New Riders offers a complete line of test preparation materials to help you achieve your certification. With books like the *MCSE Training Guide*, *TestPrep*, and *Fast Track*, and software like the acclaimed *MCSE Complete* and the revolutionary *ExamGear*, New Riders offers comprehensive products built by experienced professionals who have passed the exams and instructed hundreds of candidates.

Books for Networking Professionals

Windows NT Titles

Windows NT TCP/IP
By Karanjit Siyan
1st Edition
480 pages, $29.99
ISBN: 1-56205-887-8

If you're still looking for good documentation on Microsoft TCP/IP, then look no further—this is your book. Windows NT TCP/IP cuts through the complexities and provides the most informative and complete reference book on Windows-based TCP/IP. Concepts essential to TCP/IP administration are explained thoroughly and then are related to the practical use of Microsoft TCP/IP in a real-world networking environment. The book begins by covering TCP/IP architecture and advanced installation and configuration issues, then moves on to routing with TCP/IP, DHCP Management, and WINS/DNS Name Resolution.

Windows NT DNS
By Michael Masterson, Herman L. Knief, Scott Vinick, and Eric Roul
1st Edition
340 pages, $29.99
ISBN: 1-56205-943-2

Have you ever opened a Windows NT book looking for detailed information about DNS only to discover that it doesn't even begin to scratch the surface? DNS is probably one of the most complicated subjects for NT administrators, and there are few books on the market that address it in detail. This book answers your most complex DNS questions, focusing on the implementation of the Domain Name Service within Windows NT, treating it thoroughly from the viewpoint of an experienced Windows NT professional. Many detailed, real-world examples illustrate further the understanding of the material throughout. The book covers the details of how DNS functions within NT, then explores specific interactions with critical network components. Finally, proven procedures to design and set up DNS are demonstrated. You'll also find coverage of related topics, such as maintenance, security, and troubleshooting.

Windows NT Registry
By Sandra Osborne
1st Edition
550 pages, $29.99
ISBN: 1-56205-941-6

The NT Registry can be a very powerful tool for those capable of using it wisely. Unfortunately, there is little information available regarding the NT Registry due to Microsoft's insistence that their source code be kept secret. If you're looking to optimize your use of the Registry, you're usually forced to search the Web for bits of information. This book is your resource. It covers critical issues and settings used for configuring network protocols, including NWLink, PTP, TCP/IP, and DHCP. This book approaches the material from a unique point of view, discussing the problems related to a particular component and then discussing settings, which are the actual changes necessary for implementing robust solutions.

Windows NT Performance
Monitoring Benchmarking and Tuning
By Mark Edmead
and Paul Hinsberg
1st Edition
288 pages, $29.99
ISBN: 1-56205-942-4

Performance monitoring is a little like preventive medicine for the administrator: No one enjoys a checkup, but it's a good thing to do on a regular basis. This book helps you focus on the critical aspects of improving the performance of your NT system, showing you how to monitor the system, implement benchmarking, and tune your network. The book is organized by resource components, which makes it easy to use as a reference tool.

Windows NT Terminal Server and Citrix MetaFrame
By Ted Harwood
1st Edition
416 pages, $29.99
ISBN: 1-56205-944-0

It's no surprise that most administration headaches revolve around integration with other networks and clients. This book addresses these types of real-world issues on a case-by-case basis, giving tools and advice on solving each problem. The author also offers the real nuts and bolts of thin client administration on multiple systems, covering relevant issues such as installation, configuration, network connection, management, and application distribution.

Windows NT Power Toolkit
By Stu Sjouwerman and
Ed Tittel
1st Edition
900 pages, $49.99
ISBN: 0-7357-0922-X

This book is aimed squarely at power users, to guide them to painless, effective use of Windows NT both inside and outside the workplace. By concentrating on the use of operating system tools and utilities, Resource Kit elements, and selected third-party tuning, analysis, optimization, and productivity tools, this book will show its readers how to carry out everyday and advanced tasks.

Planning for Windows 2000
By Eric K. Cone, Jon
Boggs, and Sergio Perez
1st Edition
400 pages, $29.99
ISBN: 0-73570-048-6

Windows 2000 is poised to be one of the largest and most important software releases of the next decade, and you are charged with planning, testing, and deploying it in your enterprise. Are you ready? With this book, you will be. *Planning for Windows 2000* lets you know what the upgrade hurdles will be, informs you how to clear them, guides you through effective Active Directory design, and presents you with detailed rollout procedures. Eric K. Cone, Jon Boggs, and Sergio Perez give you the benefit of their extensive experiences as Windows 2000 Rapid Deployment Program members, sharing problems and solutions they've encountered on the job.

BackOffice Titles

Implementing Exchange Server

By Doug Hauger, Marywynne Leon, and William C. Wade III

1st Edition

400 pages, $29.99

ISBN: 1-56205-931-9

If you're interested in connectivity and maintenance issues for Exchange Server, this book is for you. Exchange's power lies in its capability to be connected to multiple email subsystems to create a "universal email backbone." It's not unusual to have several different and complex systems all connected via email gateways, including Lotus Notes or cc:Mail, Microsoft Mail, legacy mainframe systems, and Internet mail. This book covers all of the problems and issues associated with getting an integrated system running smoothly and addresses troubleshooting and diagnosis of email problems with an eye toward prevention and best practices.

Exchange System Administration

By Janice K. Howd

1st Edition

400 pages, $34.99

ISBN: 0-7357-0081-8

Okay, you've got your Exchange Server installed and connected; now what? Email administration is one of the most critical networking jobs, and Exchange can be particularly troublesome in large, heterogeneous environments. Janice Howd, a noted consultant and teacher with over a decade of email administration experience, has put together this advanced, concise handbook for daily, periodic, and emergency administration.

With in-depth coverage of topics like managing disk resources, replication, and disaster recovery, this is the one reference book every Exchange administrator needs.

SQL Server System Administration

By Sean Baird, Chris Miller, et al.

1st Edition

352 pages, $29.99

ISBN: 1-56205-955-6

How often does your SQL Server go down during the day when everyone wants to access the data? Do you spend most of your time being a "report monkey" for your coworkers and bosses? *SQL Server System Administration* helps you keep data consistently available to your users. This book omits introductory information. The authors don't spend time explaining queries and how they work. Instead, they focus on the information you can't get anywhere else, like how to choose the correct replication topology and achieve high availability of information.

SMS 2.0 Administration

By Michael Lubanski and Darshan Doshi

1st Edition Winter 2000

350 pages, $39.99

ISBN: 0-7357-0082-6

Microsoft's new version of its Systems Management Server (SMS) is starting to turn heads. Although complex, it allows administrators to lower their total cost of ownership and more efficiently manage clients, applications, and support operations. So if your organization is using or implementing SMS, you'll need some expert advice. Darshan Doshi and Michael

Lubanski can help you get the most bang for your buck, with insight, expert tips, and real-world examples. Darshan and Michael are consultants specializing in SMS, having worked with Microsoft on one of the most complex SMS rollouts in the world, involving 32 countries, 15 languages, and thousands of clients.

Networking Titles

Cisco Router Configuration & Troubleshooting
By **Mark Tripod**
1st Edition
300 pages, $34.99
ISBN: 0-7357-0024-9

Want the real story on making your Cisco routers run like a dream? Why not pick up a copy of *Cisco Router Configuration & Troubleshooting* and see what Pablo Espinosa and Mark Tripod have to say? They're the folks responsible for making some of the largest sites on the Net scream, like Amazon.com, Hotmail, USAToday, Geocities, and Sony. In this book, they provide advanced configuration issues, sprinkled with advice and preferred practices. You won't see a general overview on TCP/IP. They talk about more meaty issues, like security, monitoring, traffic management, and more. In the troubleshooting section, the authors provide a unique methodology and lots of sample problems to illustrate. By providing real-world insight and examples instead of rehashing Cisco's documentation, Pablo and Mark give network administrators information they can start using today.

Network Intrusion Detection: An Analyst's Handbook
By **Stephen Northcutt**
$39.99 US / $59.95 CAN
Available Now
0-7357-0868-1

Get answers and solutions from someone who has been in the trenches. Author Stephen Northcutt, original developer of the Shadow intrusion detection system and former Director of the United States Navy's Information System Security Office at the Naval Security Warfare Center, gives his expertise to intrusion detection specialists, security analysts, and consultants responsible for setting up and maintaining an effective defense against network security attacks.